THE FOUR GENIUSES
OF THE
BATTLE OF BRITAIN

THE FOUR GENIUSES
OF THE
BATTLE OF BRITAIN

Watson-Watt, Henry Royce, Sydney Camm and R.J. Mitchell

David Coles and
Peter Sherrard

Pen & Sword
AVIATION

First published in Great Britain in 2012 by
PEN & SWORD AVIATION
An imprint of
Pen & Sword Books Ltd
47 Church Street
Barnsley
South Yorkshire
S70 2AS

Copyright © David Coles and Peter Sherrard, 2012

ISBN 978-1-84884-759-0

Typeset by Concept, Huddersfield, West Yorkshire
Printed and bound in England by
the MPG Books Group Ltd.

Pen & Sword Books Ltd incorporates the Imprints of Pen & Sword Aviation, Pen & Sword Family History, Pen & Sword Maritime, Pen & Sword Military, Pen & Sword Discovery, Wharncliffe Local History, Wharncliffe True Crime, Wharncliffe Transport, Pen & Sword Select, Pen & Sword Military Classics, Leo Cooper, The Praetorian Press, Remember When, Seaforth Publishing and Frontline Publishing

For a complete list of Pen & Sword titles please contact
PEN & SWORD BOOKS LIMITED
47 Church Street, Barnsley, South Yorkshire, S70 2AS, England
E-mail: enquiries@pen-and-sword.co.uk
Website: www.pen-and-sword.co.uk

Contents

Acknowledgements

I wish to acknowledge the help I have been given by the RAF Museum, Hendon, the RAF Museum of Radar and Wikipedia. I would also like to extend my thanks to Brian Bowbrick, formerly of Vickers, for his superb guidance on critical points, and to David McKillop for his wonderful work on the photos.

David Eric Alfred Coles

Foreword

Picture the scene: a lovely warm summer's day in 1940s Hampshire. Between the railway line and the lazy curving road, the wheat in the large field is almost ripe and ready to harvest but it has been spoilt by tank tracks. The tank crews are resting, and the local women have come out to offer tea to these men in their machines, which are emblazoned with the empty German crosses. Thankfully these girls are not fraternizing with the enemy, and it is not what an observant small boy makes of the bizarre scene. This is an exercise and the tanks are testing the British forces to make sure they are ready for the real thing, the German invasion. The Nazis gave the planned incursion the codename *Seelöwe* (Sea Lion). It was the first planned since Napoleon's time, but never happened.

But why was that? The reason was that a small band of men and women stood in the Germans' way. But even before those few British had been called to arms, four geniuses had prepared the means for these young heroes to keep the German forces out of our country, but they only had very little time to spare!

In truth, they set an example for patriotic men and women to follow, as they readied themselves to do the best for their country, and left the tired tortoises to criticize and carp from the shelter of their homes. May there always be many such fine folk, even in our day, to lead our country! The work of these fine men carried us through the whole war, and to victory over every vicious man and machine the Nazis could throw at us. But who were these four geniuses, the giants of those days?

There are unexplained mysteries in our recent history that need exploring. Instead of moaning about wrongs and omissions, let's be surprised and truly delighted about the brilliant things that were done, when it was so easy for lazy folk or untutored financiers to strangle them at birth? Surely this ought to have a bearing on what we as a nation can do nowadays! So, let's look at our history again.

If the Merlin, Spitfire, Hurricane and radar had reached no further than 'back of envelope' ideas, the days of our young folk would have been overloaded with a barely opposed German invasion and subsequent compulsory involvement in an awful fascist youth movement, led by German overlords. What place or prospect would there have been then for a Jew or anyone else with an independent mind?

Why should our fine predecessors, Royce, Mitchell, Camm and Watson-Watt, have developed the Merlin, the Spitfire, the Hurricane and radar as private ventures, when their organizations were already successful with the Kestrel engine, flying boats, the Fury biplane, and esoteric Radio Frequency (RF) schemes? When Royce made such superb quality cars, why should he have spent money on a radically new aero engine? And why should Mitchell push a new monoplane? Supermarine was already busy with top-rate flying boats. Why did Camm leave the biplane remit? Wasn't our front-line fighter, the Hawker Fury, fast enough for the RAF? One answer is that in every decade our present aircraft are always good enough to the casual observer – so why waste money on further developments? As for radar, Watson-Watt might just as well have gone to an academic establishment in the USA. You just could not understand his technical stuff, let alone put public money into it!

These men and their small groups of assistants must have pushed very hard to get anywhere in the culture of recession, ignorance and pacifism. You can understand the prevailing attitude, exemplified in a much later cartoon where a prehistoric man says to a wheel salesman, 'I can't eat it, I can't wear it, and it costs too much!' But much more serious than that, C.E.M. Joad proposed the resolution in an infamous Oxford Union Society debate 'Under no circumstance will this House fight for King and Country', and it was passed. It was as good as any public invitation to Hitler, and it told him that our British nation was totally degenerate. Not much better in the technical field was the opinion of one RAF officer of air rank who observed that retractable landing gear was impracticable. And that was just before the coming of the DC-2, which became the DC-3, the world famous Dakota!

Just think about the results of a successful German invasion of Britain! We would have had no choice but to be a subservient part of Hitler's empire. The Nazis wouldn't have stopped at terror and repression, but would have stripped everything from Britain (food, materials and machine tools, the lot), just as they did in every other part of occupied Europe. They would have split our workforce into two groups, collaborators and slave labour. There would have been no liberty or freedom of expression. If our country had only men of small minds running the show in the 1930s, then we would have fallen with Poland and France to the Nazis.

We must credit Neville Chamberlain, Churchill's predecessor, for playing for time. Prior to his infamous negotiations with Hitler, Chamberlain as Chancellor of the Exchequer in the early 1930s had the foresight to make a greater investment in fighters rather than bombers, as they were obviously far more essential to Britain's Home Defence and in line with the concepts of Air Marshal Hugh Dowding, Air Member for Supply and Research, as opposed to Air Marshal Trenchard who supported the use of bombers.

In the Spanish Civil War General Franco used the German *Luftwaffe* to destroy the undefended Spanish city of Guernica in April 1937. From this time onwards Dowding further reinforced his opinions as he strongly argued that Britain must be able to defend itself against German bombers. He pushed for the development and manufacturing of radar and the Merlin-engined monoplanes, the Hurricane and Spitfire. These four developments combined to give the British an adequate warning of an enemy attack and the means to repulse it. Both Chamberlain and Dowding completely understood that we could only go from defence to the offensive if we had first won as defenders. Suppose that Dowding and his fellow Air Marshal, Keith Park, had been ridiculed and dismissed for their support of re-armament; it is arguable that Britain would then have been defeated by the *Luftwaffe* in 1940. What now would be our answer to that question – to re-arm or not? Today's penny-pinching politicians' answer would have led us to utter defeat.

The historic view of Chamberlain as an appeaser has changed to that of realist, a man with a steely edge to his character. He was not the completely soft and easily deceived English gentleman that Hitler despised. But with that he did not start the Second World War, using the Sudetenland crisis on 24 April 1938, so he gained our four great geniuses another sixteen valuable months by his obvious appeasement. Hitler initiated the Sudetenland crisis as part of his *Drang nach Osten* (Drive to the East). German and Austria had merged, but Czechoslovakia was a large foreign salient poking between them, so he wanted to take it over. He split this take-over into two parts, firstly by taking the Sudetenland, a mountainous region populated by Germans. Once this was done, it was easy to enter the rest of Czechoslovakia, as its natural defences were no longer Czech but German. Chamberlain and Hitler resolved this at a conference in Munich without Czech approval. This happened before the invasion of Poland moved Chamberlain to declare war on Germany, as it was obvious Hitler could never be trustworthy, but would continue eastward German expansion.

Even in the negotiations leading up to the Munich Agreement in September 1938, he refused to be bullied by Hitler as others had been. But in this he had to accept the suppression of the Czechs, and that was his stop-line. From this standpoint he later had to lead us to war in September 1939 after the German aggression against Poland. He then knew that German appetite for further territory was totally insatiable, with its start of the *Drang nach Osten* – the pressure for eastward expansion. But even with that breathing space our fine future leader, Churchill, would have been completely powerless later if he had not been given the tools to finish the job of defeating the Germans. These four geniuses were then better able to give him the means to fight, as Chamberlain had given them more time.

So now let's find out why each one of the four was the focus in his field, pulling in his supporters, whether superiors in status or members of his workforce. This focus line in turn became the volcanic fault line that broke the German plans for victory in Britain, and ultimately thwarted their thrust without parallel for world domination. All four of these men contributed to the final defeat of the Nazis, though Mitchell and Royce had died well before the start of the Second World War. We can't place one higher than another. The Bible puts it well in a different context, 'If the Whole Body were an Eye, Where is the Hearing?' In other words, each one of those four men, great in their time, had the brilliant ability and the drive to develop each concept and the equipment necessary from its very basic elements, which they then combined to form that cohesive entity, in time for the best defence possible for Britain in the crisis to come.

The first need for RAF pilots was to meet the enemy on their terms, at their height and at their speed. Watson-Watt's radar gave them the time to be there; Royce gave them the engine power to get there; Camm and Mitchell gave them the state-of-the-art machines, the Hurricane and Spitfire, to fly to meet and beat our enemy!

So radar was the 'Eye', directing these finest machines, the Hurricanes and Spitfires conceived by Camm and Mitchell, and powered by Royce's superb new aero engine, the Merlin. This book gives a new slant on 1930s history! Against all odds these Four Geniuses finely mastered its canvas, its colour, the light and the vibrance of its mature entity, which developed further with time and reached great heights in its brilliant unity!

David E.A. Coles

Preface

When David Coles outlined his planned book on the 'Four Great Men' I thought this would be an intriguing new approach to the Battle of Britain story that has been covered by many other authors. I was delighted when he suggested I should write the chapters on 'Royce and the Merlin' and 'Mitchell and the Spitfire'. I expected the former would be fairly easy as I lecture on the life of Royce. However, the lecture virtually finishes with the death of Royce in 1933 with just a brief outline of events up to the beginning of the Second World War and the Battle of Britain. It soon became evident that although Royce had produced a range of superb aero engines and had recruited an extraordinary team of engineers, by the time that he sanctioned the production of the Merlin his health had deteriorated to the extent that his input was limited to the approval of the drawings. Nevertheless, without him it is highly likely that there would not have been an engine for Mitchell's Schneider Trophy S.6 or S.6b machines, the Spitfire and all the other Merlin-powered aircraft. The development of the Merlin and the successive increases in its power throughout the war were the work of his team and, in particular, Ernest Hives. It was Hives who suggested to Royce that there was a need for a 1,000hp engine and his practical skills, foresight and rapport with the Air Ministry were absolutely essential in the success of the engine. Beaverbrook called him 'the Churchill of the Aero Engine Industry'.

I had the pleasure of meeting Hives in the 1950s when I was running one of the airflow research rigs at the Rolls-Royce Derby factory. We were testing transonic compressor blade forms and recording the shock waves on a rather 'Heath Robinson' photographic system involving a mercury vapour lamp, Gillette razor blades for the optical knife edges and a 35mm Retina SLR camera to record the results. Hives and his retinue arrived unannounced as the much more expensive, purpose-built, rig had failed during his visit. He was delighted with his first sight of supersonic shock waves and praised our rig, 'This is more like it, a typical millwright's lash up which does an effective job.'

The Mitchell chapter was a much harder task. I knew of this remarkable man and his Schneider Trophy success (I was present at the 1931 race but at the age of eleven months I did not register anything!) and, of course, his design of the Spitfire. As I researched his life I became aware that this was a man who constantly pushed the boundaries of technology, to the extent of one or two failures. He also possessed the ability to come up with quick simple fixes for problems as in the Schneider Trophy races. There is no doubt that in his relatively short career he made an enormous contribution to the aviation industry in general. Who knows what his achievements would have been had he survived. There were some similarities with Royce, as both men overcame the burden of a colostomy, and both were hard working, although, unlike the 'workaholic' Royce, Mitchell did have time for family, social and sporting activities. There is no doubt that his loss at such a young age was tragic but like Royce he had built up a highly skilled team, led by Joe Smith, to carry on his work.

Peter D. Sherrard

Chapter 1

Robert Watson-Watt – Radar's Inventor

'A man's a man for a' that.' Burn's poem well describes Robert Watson-Watt, the major inventor of radar. He was born at 5 Union Street in Brechin on 13 April 1892, one of three sons of a carpenter. He did not start out as a member of the upper crust; but from his early days he reached out for all he was given, to impart his knowledge to others in turn. His father may have expected that Robert would follow in his footsteps and work in the family business, as many other Scots have done. But Robert showed a great interest in science and looked more likely to follow in the footsteps of his famous far distant ancestor, James Watt, the inventor of the steam engine.

As a child he loved and respected his family, gaining their regard as he went to a fine school, Brechin High. He later remembered his teacher Bessie Mitchell as one 'who did more than any other teacher to make me whatever I am'. He did well there and won a scholarship to University College, Dundee, to study engineering. He graduated with a BSc (Eng.) and was offered a position with Professor William Peddie, who introduced Robert to the seemingly never-ending possibilities of radio waves. While at Dundee, Robert met a Perth girl, Margaret Robertson, who was studying art at Dundee Technical College. They married in 1916 and Margaret became an important part of Robert's radio wave experiments, when he used her skills as a jewellery maker to repair his wireless apparatus. She was a responsible, well educated lady, who transcribed the Morse-coded messages from Paris to the Aldershot command, passing on the radio transmissions that finally played such a part in that greatly desired Armistice Day, 11 November 1918.

Robert was fortunate having excellent mentors and he could take up one skill from another, from craft and classics to science. He was much more than that. Later he understood that Nazi *Realpolitik* focussed on unbridled power. Its unprincipled immorality and power-lust worried him so much that he later speeded up his radar program. A lesser man would have said, 'So what?'

He had a great ability to inspire a fine team of engineers and craftsmen, and he must have known the great thrill of invention, as he moved from tracking lightning to radar. His major change in direction occurred when in January 1935 H.E. Wimperis, Director of Scientific Research at the Air Ministry, questioned him on German death ray work, and Watson-Watt quickly returned a calculation from his assistant, Arnold Wilkins, showing that it was impractical. But he also mentioned in the same report that attention was being turned to the difficult, but more promising, problem of radio detection of aircraft. He submitted numerical considerations for this detection by reflected radio waves, and this ultimately led to radar, grounded in complex physics.

The concept of radar could even have been sown earlier when he found that aircraft disturbed lightning tracking. You can imagine the younger Watson-Watt saying with great heat and frustration, 'You never can track anything at 10.30 when that mail plane goes over!' Then one day he is inspired, 'Now that is a brilliant way to track aircraft! I'll put it in the logbook, in RED.' Maybe that is how Watson-Watt started to lay the practical and theoretical groundwork for radar during investigations into atmospheric disturbances. He said later 'Give them the third best to go on with; the second best comes too late; the first never comes.' That's true, and in no way nonsense. Advanced gear such as the klystron (a single resonant cavity device) came later but developers had to do the best with what they had then. By the time better ideas had arrived with their improved gear, the Germans would have overrun us. The cathode ray tube, the primitive predecessor of the TV tube, was invented during the 1920s and 1930s. Watson-Watt was also central to the development of other useful hardware such as the goniometer. Such work has its lows and highs, its frustration and blinding enlightenment, and he wasn't a stranger to these either.

What was the option if radar had never been invented? The large fixed acoustic detector was installed at Denge near Romney in Kent and, pointed at Amiens, but its range was only guaranteed for eight miles, twenty-four at best. As it was fixed, after reconnaissance the enemy could have easily by-passed it by making flank attacks up the Thames on London. We set up smaller steerable detectors, as well as mobile army units with range less than the larger fixed unit and its optimized design, but what a hope! Our aircraft would have barely left the ground before the Germans were upon them. It must be remembered that war is not a sport!

Then there were the death ray and ignition killer concepts. The cover of a novel from the 1930s showed a flight of enemy aircraft falling over the edge of an invisible cliff of air. In reality you needed to reach the power and frequency of radio waves required to do one or the other. Death ray equipment would kill its operators if any power leakage occurred, and it was virtually impractical before any suitable hardware evolved. A death ray at a level then attainable would have barely given an enemy pilot a headache, but it might have warmed him up. Lasers weren't invented, so there were no practical means of stopping enemy aircraft, other than shooting them down. You have to find them to do that. This then would require us to deploy standing patrols with their high pilot and aircraft wastage, and need for massive fuel stocks. The Germans then held all the initiatives to mount an airborne offensive from any point of their choosing. At the same time their submarines would be able to sink the tankers bringing in our oil supplies. Standing patrols would overload our resources in the most even-handed battle. We could reach no better than stalemate then, unable to continue and conclude the future war.

So we had to wipe the slate clean and start again. If we hadn't got an answer ready, then we couldn't possibly respond in an emergency.

In 1932 our Prime Minister, Stanley Baldwin said, 'The bomber will always get through.' But not all the British Air Ministry felt that was inevitable. In June 1934, an Air Ministry official, A.P. Rowe, went through the plans for British air defence, and was horrified to learn that our aircraft were being improved, but little was done to come up with a broad defensive strategy. Rowe wrote to his boss, Henry Wimperis, telling him that inadequate planning was likely to prove catastrophic. Wimperis took the memo very seriously and went on to propose that the Air Ministry must look into new technology for defence against air attacks. He suggested that a committee should be led by Sir Henry Tizard, a prestigious Oxford-trained chemist, the rector of Imperial College of Science and Technology. So a new 'Committee for the Scientific Survey of Air Defence' (CSSAD) was directed by Tizard, with Wimperis as a member and Rowe as secretary. Wimperis also independently investigated other possible new military technologies.

The Air Ministry had a standing prize of £1,000 to be awarded to anyone building a death ray that could kill a sheep at 200 yards. Hindsight makes the idea seem silly, but some British officials were worried that the Germans were working on such weapons, and Britain couldn't afford to be left behind. Some studies were conducted on intense radio and microwave beams, on the lines of modern 'electromagnetic pulse' weapons. Wimperis contacted Robert Watson-Watt, then head of the National Radio Research Laboratory, regarding death rays. A cheery, tubby man, Watson-Watt was highly intelligent and full of drive, but with a tendency to talk at length in a one-sided fashion. His most important ability was that he had developed a radio and triangulation system to locate thunderstorms, a most useful transferable skill.

After some informal studies and consultations with members of his lab, Watson-Watt told Wimperis that he thought death rays were impractical. However, he added that he could detect enemy aircraft by bouncing radio beams off them. Wimperis realized that such a concept worked well within the CSSAD's mandate, and put the idea to the committee members. They were interested, and in response Watson-Watt fleshed out his ideas in a memo dated 12 February

1935. He invented radar, faced with the problem of enemy aircraft detection. Only four years later his system tracked the incoming *Luftwaffe* far out to sea. Watson-Watt and Arnold Wilkins brilliantly drew up the radar document; 'brainstorming' at its best, well before the word existed.

Detection of the enemy is essential to his destruction. This starts with irradiating an aircraft with a radio beam, which makes it act like a 'half-wave' element. A voltage then develops along the largest part of the aircraft and induces a current in it, which generates a return signal. But your detector receiving the echo has to be tuned softly or you may detect a bomber but not a fighter. There are other problems if you persist in sharp tuning. If the aircraft turns then it appears to shorten and may vanish altogether, as the demodulated return signal then decreases sharply. But soften the tuning with a shunt resistor and there you are, as I remember proving for myself at RAF Locking.

The document considered so many things essential to a practical radar system, such as the measurement of the range of the target aircraft and its presentation. The first element is a transmitter feeding an aerial sending out pulses like a floodlight; it also triggers receiver circuitry. Watson-Watt used the cathode ray tube he had for ten years, showing the target as a vertical pulse shifting from its X-axis line at a distance along its face shown by range markers. The distance to the target is proportional to the return time of the transmitted beam (10.74 micro-seconds per statute mile). Right from the start he set 190 miles as a useful range for his system. Range is essential, but where is the target? So he had to find the target's bearing and height to define its position in 3-D. Bearing can be aligned to the receiver aerial system by a goniometer adjusted for its accurate return of direction. An easy way to find the target height is to get the target's elevation above horizontal, and apply maths to the range. Correct this for the earth's curvature and there you are! He considered every way to get answers to the problems presented to him, such as continuous wave and frequency change techniques.

Next he proposed IFF (Identification Friend or Foe) to discriminate between RAF and *Luftwaffe* aircraft. IFF seems a luxury, but it was really essential. Our fighters may have been alerted to shoot down an unidentified aircraft in our skies, putting a lone RAF pilot in jeopardy. Conversely, a German pilot may have roamed around British skies at will. Our radar triggered the IFF secondary pulse transponder in a British aircraft, which showed that by its modified radar plot that it was friendly. Finally, Watson-Watt appreciated the need for RAF Ground Control, as that followed radar naturally in the development of an operationally simple system. The assembled plots on a large map allowed ground controllers to discriminate easily between German and RAF flights using our later VHF radio link. Working in parallel with IFF, Ground Control could then call up a patrol to deal with a German attack shown on the map, in ideal conditions anywhere in Southern Britain. So standing patrols ceased to be needed, and that solved a frightening problem. The Observer Corps used high grade binoculars to identify enemy aircraft numbers and types, to complete the picture. With modern day technology you could do that with radar as well, but in those days the Observer Corps gave us the immediate, low-tech answer and final piece in the jigsaw!

In all these advances, Watson-Watt was ably helped both by his superiors, among them Tizard and Lord Swinton, and his own team including Rowe and Wilkins. But without his leadership and drive, little of this could have happened. His team was so small that it was overloaded in dealing with all the ideas it conceived.

With this foresight, Watson-Watt was brilliant in his anticipation of what was needed. Later he analysed his dependence on his radio predecessors, Henry Jackson in Britain, Heinrich Hertz and Christian Hulsmeyer in Germany, and Guglielmo Marconi in Italy. These were the 'Prior Artists', but Watson-Watt took the critical onward steps from their basic ideas. From his experience he knew that the electromagnetic spectrum properties were not cohesively unified. Typically, radio waves cease to be reflected between the earth and the ionosphere at higher radio frequencies, when they disappear into space. To reach a new realm of thought and come up with a new patent, there must be a need for new techniques and hardware, at that point to stop a coming German invasion. The hardware was there or nearly so, and he used it to implement many new techniques to bring radar to fruition.

The CSSAD was enthusiastic about radar, but had to move from paper ideas to demonstrate the concept before the Air Ministry granted development cash. So the starting point in British radar history was the demonstration held in Daventry prepared by Watson-Watt and his team before dawn on 26 February 1935, successfully proving that radar could detect aircraft, to the satisfaction of all the civil servants and RAF officers involved, Dowding in particular. So now radio waves would spot planes!

The demonstration used the 10kW Daventry short wave transmitter, operating not in pulse mode but in continuous wave mode at 6MHz (50 metres). At the aerial site in a field south of Weedon, seven miles from the transmitter, the amplified outputs of two horizontally polarized receiving aerials, pointing towards it, were first adjusted on a CRT (cathode ray tube) to give a null signal when no aircraft were present. These aerials were fixed to two 15 feet high posts, 50 feet apart, set on a straight line joining the transmitter, aerial 1 and aerial 2. The CRT gave a well defined signal when Squadron Leader R.S. Blucke flew the Heyford bomber shown, over the line extending between the transmitter and receivers to 20 miles out from the transmitter, at a height of 6,000 feet. So detection using radio waves worked and radar was viable, at that time not using the pulse techniques much loved by the author, but this was a real start and no mistake! It was brilliantly done using existing gear such as the Daventry transmitter. Even the receivers were simply modified existing equipment – it must have taken only a day to modify one of them for the test. This was done frugally; the most expensive part of the demonstration would have been the Heyford flight! Watson-Watt was so heavily involved in discussion after the demonstration he completely forgot to pick up his twenty-three-year-old nephew at the finish! He was so impressed that he said, 'Britain has become an island again!'

Dowding now made radar 'MOST SECRET', and backed the project to the tune of £12,300, then a massive sum, for development of the new radio echo detection system.

At the Daventry demonstration an Air Ministry man observed, 'It was demonstrated beyond doubt that electro-magnetic energy is reflected from the metal components of an aircraft's structure and that it can be detected.' Later the Scientific Survey of Air Defence group stated, 'The result was much beyond expectation.' The RAF officers there could have sat on their hands and said, 'What a scheme! It's a pity we can't afford it!' Instead they spent millions of pounds and saved their country from a bitter defeat at the hands of the Germans. But in the words of Wellington at Waterloo, our future victory in the air was 'a damned close run thing!'

Another facet in Watson-Watt's character appeared from this time onwards, the ability to keep his mouth shut. This was hard for a man more used to broadcasting success. His awareness of the degeneration of the German psyche, from the start of the Nazi regime, made him accelerate the progress of radar development. He completely understood what was needed of a radar system – detection, ranging, direction-finding, height-finding and, finally, reporting. The importance of reporting was later shown by its horrific failure at Pearl Harbor in 1941, when a junior radar operator saw that a large force was approaching without notification, but somehow his warning of the Japanese raid did not reach his senior officers. So, if reporting failed, then its failure made the whole system useless. After that, you can't blame Watson-Watt's recognition of his own self-worth; or as the Scots would put it, he had 'a Guid Conceit o' Himsel'.

Early radar – Chain Home (CH)

Radar was well on its way. After intense brainstorming, late night sessions, and hard work, Watson-Watt's team, notably including Arnold Wilkins and Edward Bowen, developed a working pulsed radar system in June 1935. The transmitter array consisted of two tall towers with antenna wires strung between them, while the receiver array consisted of two similar arrays arranged in parallel. The number of arrays was increased later, but now an exercise at Bawdsey gave nine reports per hour on 18 September 1936, improving to 124 in 115 minutes, six days later. The first five bi-static Chain Home (CH) radar stations at Bawdsey, Canewdon, Dover, Dunkirk, and Great Bromley were completed by July 1938, ready for the August 1938 exercise. Their transmitters and receivers were separated by about 300 yards at bi-static stations.

Range

The CH system schematic diagram on the next page shows the RAF radar system driving the Synchronizing Pulse Generator (Sync. Pulse Gen.). If the RAF system was damaged, the Sync. Pulse Gen., the radar station master circuit, oscillated in a free running mode. Ideally, interference between our radar stations could be minimized by using mains synchronization or a national 400Hz source via land lines. Each radar station realistically needs its own back-up power and synchronization in readiness for battle conditions. In either case its 400Hz p.r.f. (pulse repetition frequency) pulse output triggered the Transmitter Power Driving Circuit and Array to send the radar pulse. It also started the time-base and range marker generators. The target aircraft reflected the radar pulse back to the receiver array and receiver circuit, whose output was fed to the CRT 'Y' plates as a negative pulse. The range markers were fed to the 'Y' plates as a series of positive pulses. The time base generator applied a linearly increasing voltage to the CRT 'X' plates giving the return time. This all showed the range of the target aircraft in a manner fast understood by the operator.

The system range depends on its p.r.f. and other factors, as shown in the diagram.

Bearing

The next data required from the system was the target bearing. CH transmission had a direction with the most pulse energy, the Line of Shoot. Aligned to the 'shoot', the aerial on the receiver tower comprised two pairs of horizontally aligned crossed dipoles. Each pair was fitted at a mean height of 215 feet, 5 feet either side of the centre-line, set mutually at right angles to each other.

Wilkins installed reflecting dipoles behind both main dipole sets. These could be switched to resolve ambiguity between seaward and landward directions, an essential requirement; otherwise operators

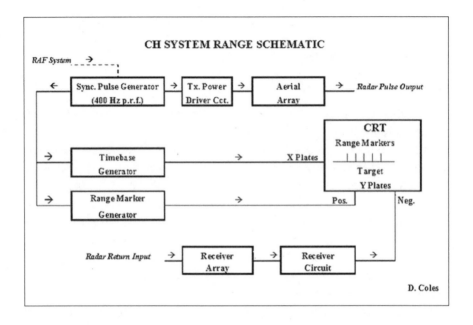

would puzzle 'Where on earth is Jerry?' The outputs of the main dipoles fed the operator's goniometer via cables, set mutually at right angles, to give the target bearing on a search coil feeding a CRT. A second search coil, 90° to the first, improved bearing accuracy as it was used to find the null return.

Height finding

Height was found using two antenna groups, fixed at heights of 45 and 95 feet on the one hand, and 95 and 215 feet on the other, to establish two different lobe angles. The receiver data gave the target's elevation above horizontal between 1½° and 16°. This was then combined with range data to give height. Wilkins worked on the scheme before Daventry, as it was completely essential to height finding. An electrical calculator used relays and stepping relays, to simplify CH calculations from 1940.

CH transmitters worked best at 23MHz. But the type R3020 could select one of four frequency groups, 20–30MHz, 22–36MHz,

28-42MHz and 32–46MHz. This reduced the system's vulnerability to jamming, a threat that was taken seriously right at the start.

CH systems floodlit an area to the front of the transmitter with a horizontal beam width of 60°. Horizontal polarization was used in CH as it was the best way to detect a bomber seen as a resonant half-wave element. Horizontal antennas generated this polarization mode, fed via balanced open-wire feeders, completely symmetrical about earth, in turn fed by high voltage push-pull transmitter output valves. Old radar fitters will remember high voltage gear painted a vivid red, warning them to keep them away from lethal equipment. Close by there was a cartoon of an electrocuted fitter smashing through a wall. Seriously, a further advantage of horizontal polarization was immunity from sea clutter, which worsened in frequent storms at the more common coastal sites.

CH used complex transmitter arrays carried on steel towers, each array a curtain of dipoles and reflectors between towers, to give the best vertical beam spread with the least gaps. Receivers were fitted to wooden towers about 300 yards away. Spark gap/transmission line units stopped transmitter power entering the receiver system, preventing damage or overload. Work started on-site after a survey reached the best compromise between height, ground load-bearing, and local acceptance. Petrol engines were barred near receivers on active sites. You can visualize their interference if you recall un-suppressed ignition's effect on 405-line TV sets later in peacetime! Finally, the site was calibrated accurately using a stationary target such as an autogyro.

CRT display – X-Y and PPI

Watson-Watt first used the CRT in his lightning instrumentation at Slough in 1920. This showed time horizontally and the signal vertically, as an 'X-Y' display. Distance was found by comparing displays from two separated stations by triangulation. Watson-Watt's colleague, J.F. Herd, applied the input from one station to the X-trace and the input from a second station to the Y-trace, and combined the signals to indicate the direction of the common signal from a lightning strike.

When Bowen later planned the AI and ASV systems at Bawdsey, he developed radar systems with rotatable antennas, and the display could map target location precisely.

Such a display was again considered for CHL (Chain Home Low), a different concept to CH on two counts, firstly where the radar operator's time-base started from the centre of the CRT, rotating round it like the spokes of a wheel in synchronism with the antenna direction. Secondly, this antenna was a rotating 32-dipole aerial array working at a higher frequency, giving a narrower beam, both in direction and elevation. This detected aircraft at a lower altitude, and operationally improved CH stations with their companion CHL. The target signal registered when it coincided with this revolving line. This was called the 'Radial Time Base' (RTB). Some work on this was done by the CHL team but, since the initial system used two antennas and they were hand-rotated, the display work was unfortunately made low priority.

Albert Percival Rowe and Wilfrid Bennett Lewis saw that the RTB could be used in a station with common antennas for transmitting and receiving, to give a sharply focussed rotating lighthouse-like beam. This was turned into hardware when in 1940 Geoffrey Dummer at Dundee was chosen to lead display development. GEC and EMI jointly developed 50cm (600MHz) transmitters and receivers with rotating antennas, which were used to test the display. The RTB development made good progress but there was little progress in the matching radar equipment.

A new type of CRT with a long persistence screen was necessary to make the target spot image remain for a complete rotation of the display. This was finally achieved by using two different phosphors – one of low persistence to quickly indicate the target with a blue flash, and a second one with an orange afterglow activated by the initial flash. To emphasize the pattern sustaining glow, a filter pass-ing the orange colour was placed in front of the CRT face. The trace showed up just like a tadpole on the tube and so its movement showed the target manoeuvres and direction.

After the move to Swanage in May 1940, the 600MHz radar was still not completed, but the display was ready for testing. Dummer then coupled the display to a 200MHz CHL set with a revolving antenna, showing that the scheme was satisfactory during the summer of 1940. In September it impressed Sir Philip Joubert, Assistant Chief of Air Staff of Coastal Command, who ordered it to be adopted. The new display was soon called Plan Position Indicator (PPI) in our Ground Controlled Interception (GCI) stations; and the concept was developed independently by the British, Germans and Americans once they had each fully developed such devices as duplexers, T/R cells and common rotating antennas. The T/R cell is a gas discharge tube that shorts the receiver input by switching on during the transmitted pulse so protecting the receiver. The transmitted pulse causes the gap in the cell to break down, which becomes a short circuit. But gas discharge tubes take time to turn on, and longer to turn off. So an extra electrode in the cell makes it ready for action by feeding it a small current. The gas in the cell is critical to the time it takes for it to ionize and de-ionize. Water vapour is the best and the most stable.

A useful development later was the Photographic Display Unit or PDU, which projected PPI information on to a large screen above, in the GCI Control Centre.

This was used in parallel with a console for each individual radar operator. These consoles incorporated the superbly elegant fixed coil system, which replaced the old rotating coil scheme. This had previously used a coil rotating round the neck of the tube, but now the fixed coil scheme used stationary coils in its place, still working when I was in the RAF in 1957. Added to that was the video map, superimposing an outline of Britain from a high contrast slide, on the radar display.

The coming of mono-static radar

Prefixes, such as bi, mono, pseudo-mono, stated that transmitter and receiver aerials on site were apart (bi-static); one-piece (mono-static); or close (pseudo-mono-static).

New components now allowed mono-static radar to be used with its ultimate accuracy.

True mono-static radar has one common antenna, which is switched over from the transmitter to the receiver. The transmitter pulse power must be high as the outgoing signal from the antenna travels out two hundred miles, reflects from the target aircraft, returns the same distance to the antenna, and finally enters the receiver. Even the best processed signal is heavily reduced in the process, so in all cases the sequence must be:

1. The transmitter powers the antenna for a very short time, and then shuts down.
2. Then antenna and receiver 'look' a thousand times longer for the returning pulse.

To make this work a duplexer switches between transmitter and receiver, so that:

a. The receiver only absorbs little of the transmitter power during 'transmit' time.
b. The receiver is not damaged by the power it absorbs.
c. Its sensitivity recovers immediately after 'transmit' time to see targets close in.
d. The transmitter only absorbs a very small part of the returning signal power.

The common antenna is connected to the transmitter during 'transmit' time, switching to the receiver for the 'receive' time. Relays, switching 1 watt in 1mS (1 milli-second), demonstrate this at low frequencies, but they are useless practically as radar output power is about a mega-watt; and 'out-and-back' time for a mile is 10μS (10 microseconds). 1mS accounts for about 100 miles, blinding a radar up to this distance close to home. The system timing will be inaccurate anyway, so the concept appears useless. But microwave devices, quenched by avalanche components, can unite in the design of this essential switch. Microwaves surprise students with interesting steel quarter-wave stub 'insulators' for transmission lines. Just as a brake was copied for a car clutch, so microwave concepts could be used in different ways for radar. These are obvious starts for duplexer design.

There are many ways to design a duplexer, so the diagram shows how it all goes together and how it works. Firstly there are the

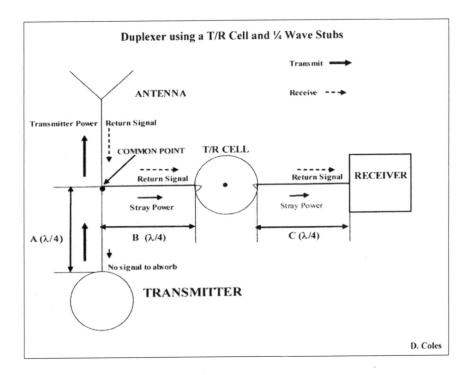

Duplexer using a T/R Cell and ¼ Wave Stubs

D. Coles

common elements, the radar antenna, the transmitter, the T/R cell and the receiver. These are linked by quarter-wave stubs, using co-axial cable or waveguide.

The diagram shows the duplexer in both 'transmit' and 'receive' modes. The 'light arrows' are titled 'Stray Power', the leakage going towards the receiver – this must be kept small by the T/R cell or else the receiver won't last two minutes! The 'dashed arrows' are titled 'Return Signal' coming from the target aircraft, and that takes the path, Antenna – Common Point – T/R Cell – Receiver (this signal must not be reduced between Antenna and Receiver). The transmitter circuit effectively controls everything, as it powers the antenna, shown by the heavy arrows going from transmitter to the antenna, but some energy escapes at the common point via the branch to the receiver, which it would damage. But between this point and the receiver there is a quarter-wave stub (B), the T/R cell and a second quarter-wave stub (C), the same length as B. The stray energy is sufficient to cause the T/R cell to oscillate and avalanche, with a pale blue glow. The impedance of the cell is now a low value, and the first quarter-wave stub (B) appears as a high impedance at the common point. The reduced power level at the cell's low output impedance appears at the input of the second quarter-wave stub (C), which now presents high impedance at the receiver circuit, reducing leakage power to a low, safe level.

As the transmitter becomes quiescent it starts the 'receive' period. The target signal returning from the antenna passes to the common point. The first quarter-wave stub (B), the inert T/R cell and the second quarter-wave stub (C) combine as a single half-wave circuit of low impedance between the common point and the receiver. This passes the total energy from the antenna to the receiver. The quiescent transmitter's low output impedance now presents high impedance via the quarter-wave stub (A) to the common point, so the transmitter does not abstract any return signal energy, and the receiver is given the whole return signal.

CHL, CHEL and AI – Watson-Watt and Bowen
Rotating aerial systems arrived later in 1941 with CHL, the pseudo mono-static Chain Home Low, primitive in its early days when the operator aligned the receiver to the transmitter by following an indicator. Results were improved by switching the receiver antenna side lobes either side of the true aiming point. The pulse looking to one side is amplified. Seen on a CRT, when the receiver array is spot-on with the true bearing, the two pulses side by side are equal. This improves bearing accuracy by a factor of 20, from 2° to 0.1°. The Germans also coded side lobes differently in the mid-1930s.

CHL was followed by the mono-static Chain Home Extra Low (CHEL). Here the new duplexer and T/R cell circuit allowed the radar output pulse and its return pulse to share a common antenna without damaging the receiver, shown in the scheme above.

This was operational in 1942 when the advent of 10cm wavelengths made it feasible. At the start of radar development in 1936, it was obvious that the Germans would move to night bombing if a daylight offensive did not achieve results. Watson-Watt therefore charged Bowen with developing Airborne Interception (AI) radar, to be installed in a fighter. Bowen was given AI specification limits of 200lb weight, 8 cubic feet volume, 500 watts power, and a 1.5-metre wavelength to reduce antenna drag to a minimum. A working AI unit was first air-tested in a Heyford bomber at the end of 1937, then further developed, tested and miniaturized in the Anson, Battle, Blenheim and Hudson. The system was perfected by 1940, installed in the Beaufighter and ended the Blitz in 1941.

AI was a brilliantly miniaturized equivalent of ground CHL and CHEL radars. It was a mini-radar station in the sky, totally essential for operations against German night raiders.

Here our Ground Radar station used both height and PPI data to show the positions of the enemy bomber and our IFF equipped night fighter, to bring the bomber ahead to within our fighter's AI range limit. Its AI could then take over, bridging the gap between Ground Radar and the fighter pilot's visual limit at night of about 300 yards.

With the start of the Second World War on 3 September 1939, CH and the other systems were used in anger. CH was used from the Munich Crisis in 1938 until the end of the Second World War.

ASV and other developments

Bowen also developed anti-submarine radar, ASV (Air to Surface Vessel), installed in Coastal Command flying boats. Now they sank six times as many U-boats, rising to twelve per year. With the later ASV Mk VI, aircrews in these Sunderlands deceived U-boats with a superb ruse. On finding a U-boat, they reduced ASV transmitter power and deceived its crew into thinking the aircraft was leaving the target area. It didn't always go the RAF's way as a U-boat could put up a blistering ack-ack (anti-aircraft fire). To avoid 'friendly fire' between Coastal Command British submarines, the submarine HMS *Unbeaten* was the first fitted with aircraft radar and IFF (Interrogation Friend or Foe) in September 1942. In spite of IFF, on 11 November 1942, commanded by Lt Donald Eric Ogilvy Watson, RN, it was sunk in error by a Wellington of 172 Squadron, Coastal Command in the Bay of Biscay.

17

The flying boats also had to cope with Ju 88s as well, which were capable of 300mph, 60mph faster than the Sunderland. But our brave crews and good gunnery with eight angry .303s, and of course ASV, tipped the balance as the U-boats could have starved Britain out. Ju 88s needed the best aircrews even to match these 'fretful porpentines'!

The development of gun laying and proximity fuse radar also helped our defence as enemy bombers had to fly through a curtain of fire. Even against novice gun crews, the best German pilots could not give their bomb aimers an accurate run in, as they would have to jink just before bomb release. This was also experienced by our own bombers later over Germany (one RAF pilot I knew estimated the response time of the best German ack-ack, so he would jink just before their gunners could get him). So our good gun laying meant that German bombers had to fly high, up to their ceiling in fact, thus reducing their accuracy and performance, and cutting German hits on strategic targets.

Modified IFF gave our aircrews in emergencies an aiming point at their airfields. There was so much new radar equipment that ensured the British victory in 1945, but at the start of the War the Germans were only just behind us in radar development. In December 1939 their Freya and Würzburg radars detected RAF aircraft sixty miles away on their run in to Heligoland Bight. Incidentally, the codename 'Freya' was a giveaway to R.V. Jones, one of our scientists knowledgeable in Norse classics. Freya the Norse goddess looked back over the past week and forward to the next, hence our Friday. Freya radar was exactly that, forward and backward looking at the same time. The Germans could not be clever all the time, but their codename 'Würzburg' was completely neutral so it gave us no clue at all. Even if they had fully known about our radar, it still remained completely essential to us. There was some truth in British reports that the Germans had assumed that the very obvious CH towers were primarily naval. A Zeppelin had surveyed our CH stations before the war, and found no relevant data here as these had been synchronized to our power frequency via phone lines. Before international power frequency synchronization, British sync pulses would have drifted in and out of the Zeppelin monitoring system and confused it. Otherwise the German air offensive would have hit our radar stations as hard as the airfields they controlled. So the Germans assumed that radar was less important and irrelevant to our defences.

The Battle of Britain

Churchill exulted in our pilots' bravery as every day they fought off the *Luftwaffe*: 'Never in the field of human conflict was so much owed by so many to so few.'

The Battle of Britain was the most decisive battle of the Second World War. A British defeat would have let the *Luftwaffe* knock out our capital ships and stop the RAF inflicting major damage on the German invasion fleets. This would make invasion inevitable, with the Royal Navy unable to stop an easy transfer of the Wehrmacht to Britain, leading to our final defeat. But this wonderful British victory in the air was the start for all British victories. If our enemy had not been Germany, radar would have been no more than a toy, but it consigned the Nazis to the Nuremberg trials, and ultimately to History.

Our aircraft were the Spitfire and the Hurricane. The Spitfire went for their fighters, the Bf109 and Me110, and the Hurricane knocked out the more numerous He 1-11, with its supporters, the Do 17, and the Ju 88, faster by 50mph than its predecessor.

The Battle of Britain opened in earnest on 12 August 1940 with attacks on five radar stations between Dover and Ventnor. Four of these sites were repaired within six hours, so quickly that the Germans concluded they had not been hit! Only Ventnor was completely knocked out, due more to the menace of unexploded bombs, but it reopened on 23 August. At Ventnor, as in all these sites, you must remember the heroic men and women who faced the continuing blitz, many at the cost of their lives. Ventnor is now a haunted place, many years after. Walk alone past the old site at midnight when you change watch! It is just as the poet said – you can sense someone walking close behind you. Ventnor's sacrifice opened the battle in our favour, when the Germans lost thirty-six aircraft to our twenty-two. We must also refer to women radar operators. In 1937, Watson-Watt could see how women could excel as operators, so three typist secretaries were retrained. These three were the basis of the wartime operator cadre, which proved incredibly brave under fire. He referred to their discretion as 'The secret that was kept by a thousand women, kept not merely from probable foes, but from friends, families and I have no doubt from fiancés.' This was reinforced in Fougasse cartoons by Cyril Kenneth Bird, showing Hitler and a fat Goering listening on a railway luggage rack to the chat below, with the slogan 'Careless Talk Costs Lives!'

But radar was rested while the battle continued on 13 August, and it was our fighter airfields' turn to be hit. Even with a force of 1,485 aircraft, the Germans lost forty-seven to our thirteen, mainly due to a poor weather forecast.

The Germans changed tactics on 14 August when they pulled their Ju 87 'Stuka' dive-bombers out of their attack force, after heavy losses inflicted by the RAF and flak. The British found the Stuka in its dive so predictable that it was easily shot down, even if it terrified my Aunty Joyce and me. Our screams added to the racket!

Now the Germans started probing our defence's western flank, raiding the West Country. Western Britain was no easy place for them either; shown in their loss of nineteen aircraft for our eight. On 15 August, the Germans tried a two-pronged attack, again on Kent, and for the first time on the Newcastle area. Now it was the North's turn, as our radar's first estimate of 30 rose to 170 enemy aircraft, Me110s and Heinkel 1-11s. This was a serious probing attack now on our northern flank, but radar and fighters more than matched the *Luftwaffe*. No. 72 Squadron split the force; 79 Squadron severely mauled one half before they had reached the coast. The Germans turned for home, short of fuel and beaten by too much RAF attention, and 616 and 73 Squadrons caught fifty German aircraft headed for Scarborough ten miles from Flamborough Head.

A mix of German aircraft looking for targets elsewhere damaged Driffield airfield and an ammunition dump near Bridlington. The profit and loss account at the end of this Northern incursion reads 'German Bombers 24, Fighters 1; RAF 0, Driffield drome, Bridlington dump, and 24 houses in Sunderland damaged'. The loss of these houses was hard to bear, but the Germans never again tried an attack on the North East in the Battle of Britain. No, we did not strip our Northern defences to cover the South.

On 15 August the battle for the South East continued, with a three-pronged attack of 100-plus aircraft each over Bawdsey, Deal and Folkestone. Our fighters shielded our airfields, but the Germans severely damaged two aircraft factories. Further round the South coast, radar reported a total of 200-plus Germans, but most of these were beaten back in fierce fights off Portsmouth and Portland. The German weakness here was that their long flight from Normandy gave our radar a more advanced warning. Their last strike for the day was a small mixed force of Bf109s and Me110s which reached Croydon. So 15 August was the most massive trial yet, with 500 bombers and 1,300 fighters invading our airspace in five major assaults. RAF historians concluded, 'Nowhere had they discovered a serious gap in our defences' in spite of all this. The total losses for the day were Germans seventy-six and RAF thirty-four. Historically, conclusions at the German conference for the day were that the RAF and British aircraft industry had to be hit harder, but attacks on radar sites could be reduced as they had never been put out of action. Dowding had anticipated this thinking by ensuring that our radar sites kept going so the Germans would play down their importance. Goering and his officers mistakenly worked on the basis that radar was of no importance, but our historians said this was a 'Fatal, and fateful, turn of policy'. Only two more attacks were made on our radar stations, one of course on Ventnor, and the town below was blitzed as well!

On 16 August the German raids were nearly as strong, when they sent more than 1,700 aircraft. They increased their fighter numbers with more than three to each bomber, but that cautionary tactic did not stop them from losing forty-five to our twenty-one. Now the Germans were trying every trick in the book to overload our fighters and their control. They tried feint attacks, snap attacks, and decoys during major attacks. Another *Luftwaffe* ploy was to carefully time more than one major attack, originating from widely separated bases on separate targets. But Goering was now misled by optimistic reports of his light losses and heavy British losses. From 8 to 26 August the true losses were 602 German and 259 British, instead of the optimistic German figure of 353 and 791 respectively – no wonder he thought he had got us; but we had managed to widen our radar cover at that point quite adequately for all Britain except western Scotland.

CH was important to the defence of Britain, but filter rooms also played a key role in Fighter Command. With the Royal Observer Corp's confirmation of numbers and types of enemy bombers, they gained a clear picture of the threat from the numerous overlapping radar plots reported from various stations, and then matched fighter resources against the enemy. The British developed an advantage over the Germans in the way in which they used radar, this major component in the air defence picture. Spotting reports and signals intelligence filled in the areas where radar could not see, aircraft over 120 miles away and in Britain past the radar stations on the landward side.

German-speaking British controllers further confused German pilots by breaking into their frequencies. I heard that RAF and *Luftwaffe* controllers once ended up in a screaming match. That would doubly worry a *Luftwaffe* pilot, firstly because his enemy could listen to his controller, and secondly, now he did not know who to trust.

Signals intelligence was just as valuable to the British as CH radar. The British repeated their First World war naval successes in modern air combat. Excellent signals anticipated radar reports of expected approaching aircraft. CH was able to give a twenty-minute warning to the fighters to intercept their target, but radar on its own could not easily resolve aircraft numbers or types. German communications were intercepted by British High Frequency (HF) listening stations. Early in the war the German fighters used HF radio telephony while the bombers used more traditional HF telegraphy for communications. From the interception of this traffic, the British were given a two-hour warning and detailed information on aircraft numbers, routes and identity of attacking formations. It took just six minutes to dispatch fighters from the first data given to us.

CHL had also arrived to improve our picture. Further elements in our defence were the seven Sector Stations, strategically placed between the coastal Radar Stations and London. Our operation rooms were essential. But on 18 August, the hardest day yet, Kenley was the first to be heavily damaged. Forward planning enabled its 'ops' to be re-instated in a disused business in the high street. The Germans continued their attacks on these seven Home Counties airfields and Sector Stations. Biggin Hill was the worst hit, with six attacks in three days, and its 'Ops' room was also transferred to a business premises in the village on 31 August, just like Kenley before it.

The Germans fully understood that their invasion plan depended on total annihilation of the RAF. Otherwise the Great War's historic bloodbath would run again in Southern England. Both their Army and naval leaders could see this, so they were reluctant to move until Goering had defeated our Air Force. So at this stage, the date was set for invasion on 15 September, and Goering was optimistic. On 6 August he had given his senior officers four days to destroy the RAF in the South, followed by a clear-up in the North, scheduled in four weeks.

The massive fighter requirement did not force the RAF to weaken our bomber effort. On 2 July, and 12, 13 and 23 August they hit the Dortmund-Ems canal, the aorta of the German waterways running from the Ruhr to the Rhine, connecting them to the invasion ports, which were also attacked. Our Bomber Command at that stage concentrated on enemy ports and shipping at Kiel, Hamburg, Wilhelmshaven, Bremen, Rotterdam, and Brunsbüttel, as well as barges and small craft on other canals, and in the ports of Holland and Belgium. Such dislocation caused the German Navy to worry, 'If the RAF can do that here, what could they do if we invaded Britain?' When the *Luftwaffe* went for London, the RAF replied in kind and attacked Berlin itself. That deflated Goering who had said, 'You may call me Meyer if a British bomber reaches Berlin!' The Berliners later called their sirens 'Meyer Trumpets'! This attack finally exhausted the Führer's proverbial patience. He therefore deferred the invasion to 21 September, ordered a major air attack on London, and diverted the *Luftwaffe*'s attacks from the RAF airfields, which was the tactical change and relief the RAF needed. On 7 September the Thameshaven oil tank farm, the London docks and their surrounding houses were hit. For this the Germans lost thirty-eight aircraft to our twenty-eight. Terrible fires in London became a beacon in the night, and only one raider was downed. German aircrew reports magnified our loss of twenty-eight fighters, so they pressed home their attacks until 13 September. Weather reduced their intensity on 10, 12 and 13 September. Buckingham Palace was hit, and the Queen's answer to this was 'Now we can look the East End in the eye.'

On 10 September Hitler deferred the invasion for three more days. On 12 September, Grand Admiral Raeder at the German Naval HQ in Paris told him that invasion harbours between Boulogne and Ostende could not be used overnight as British air raids and long-range shelling made that impossible; and the British Navy was able to operate freely anywhere in the English Channel. So he expected the assembly of the invasion ships to be delayed and sourly commented that, for operational and military reasons, even the major German effort in the air war had not caused him to consider the invasion possible. The climax of the Battle of Britain was on 15 September, marked since as 'Battle of Britain' Day. The *Luftwaffe* command increased their fighter escort ratio to five fighters per bomber, 679 to 139. Their bombers, mostly He 1-11s, were 100mph slower than our fighters, so this massive escort was essential. As in a historic set-piece battle, they sent up an orderly force. Gathering this took time from assembly at their bases to the approach to Britain, giving the RAF time to bring up large formations and pull in reserves from every group. The RAF was ready to intercept this massive force at the coast itself, and for once it outnumbered it, scattering the tidy *Luftwaffe* air fleet, and harrying it homeward before lunch.

The *Luftwaffe* continued in the afternoon in an attempt to break the RAF, and even then they did no better. Churchill was there at this critical point in the 11 Group Ops room, and asked their leader, Air Chief Marshal Keith Park, 'What reserves have we got?' Park, with his complete grasp of strategy, replied, 'There are none!' Churchill remembered, 'Another five minutes passes, and most of our squadrons have descended to refuel. In many cases our resources could not give them overhead protection. Then it appeared that the enemy were going home.'

The Germans had more than their fill of disappointment and defeat, losing thirty-four bombers and twenty-two fighters that day. Each He 1-11, their main bomber, carried a crew of five so that meant 170 men. Include the fighter pilots and the loss is close on 200 men. This is vividly shown in the *Battle of Britain* film with a full *Luftwaffe* aircrew mess room at its start; at the end there are so many empty seats. The British had stopped the invasion of their shores, but it was extremely close. On 17 September Hitler delayed Operation *Sea Lion*, and finally called it off on 12 October until the spring of 1941.

The Battle of Britain was very costly for both sides. At the start the RAF had 1,936 serviceable aircraft and the *Luftwaffe* 2,550. The RAF lost 1,547 aircraft and the *Luftwaffe* 1,887. The RAF lost 544 aircrew and the *Luftwaffe* 2,698. What a waste of life, but our pilots bought our liberty with their lives! German lives were wasted by Adolf Hitler, and as Douglas Bader said when he heard about the terrible death of a German flyer, 'They shouldn't have been over here! 'From November 1940 the *Luftwaffe* stopped concentrating on London, and started on other towns. Raids on London were less frequent, no longer every night. But some were heavier and more explosives and incendiaries were dropped than in the earlier raids.

Hitler deferred his invasion plans again until the spring of 1942, hoping to set them up after he had defeated the Russians. So the RAF won the Battle of Britain and saved our country from an evil tyranny. It did not end there, with many more battles to come.

The London Blitz

The London Blitz was the first major strike against our civilians, and the opener with which the Germans tried to break the British people, but it continued after the end of the Battle of Britain. London was so large that the German pilots did not need fantastic navigational aids, used later to such terribly destructive effect on Coventry and other targets. Even a new aircrew fresh from training could find London – all they had to do was to fly westward from their smart new airbase in Holland.

The first big air raid on London started on 7 September and targeted industrial areas and docklands, mainly in the East End of London. For a few weeks, these raids took place day and night, but the Germans switched to night raids because they lost too many bombers in daytime. Our night defence of London was only partial. Ack-ack guns lifted Londoners' morale, but they brought down only a few bombers.

The RAF could not effectively use night fighters until AI had been produced in quantity. It stopped the Blitz on our towns and cities in 1941 when Oxford's Clarendon Laboratory completed the development of the T/R cell, and brought AI to its full potential. As shown in the description of the mono-static radar and duplexer, a high power transmitter and a vulnerable, sensitive receiver could now share one antenna, cut power losses to a negligible level, take out position error, and improve the accuracy of AI.

From mid-September 1940, after their defeat in the Battle of Britain, the *Luftwaffe* changed over to a war of attrition when they attacked the rest of London. Air raids took place almost every night and a large number of German bombers dropped hundreds of tons of bombs on the capital. Typically there were 100 to 200 bombers dropping around 200 tons of high explosive and 300 tons of incendiaries, but they occasionally raided London using 300 and 400 planes, with more than double the number of bombs dropped. These raids brought London to the brink when loss of pumps, appliances and firemen almost caused unstoppable destruction. There were terrible pictures of streets on fire shedding their frontages like waterfalls, as their red hot steel supports failed. From November 1940 the *Luftwaffe* eased up on London and started bombing other towns and cities instead. Raids on London continued but not every night. However, some raids were heavier with more High Explosive (HE) and incendiaries.

On the night of 29 December 1940 the *Daily Mail*'s chief photographer, Herbert Mason, took the iconic Second World War photograph, while firewatching on the paper's roof. The London Blitz was at its height; after a brief pause decreed by Hitler on Christmas Day, Goering's bombers resumed their almost nightly pounding on the capital. On 27 December a brief attack caused 600 casualties, fifty of them when a public shelter in Southwark received a direct hit. When night fell on 29 December, the Heinkel and Dornier bombers launched their 125th attack since the start of the campaign, which inflicted unparalleled devastation on City of London. Thirty minutes into the raid, *Luftwaffe* aircrew counted fifty-four major fires below them. In three hours of early evening bombing, 120 tons of explosive and 22,000 incendiaries fell, inflicting horrific damage. Hundreds of buildings in the finance district were set ablaze; eight Christopher Wren churches were destroyed and the fifteenth century Guildhall was set on fire. One bomb landed near the Great Fire Monument.

A middle-aged spinster named Vera Hodgson, who worked in a charity shop in Notting Hill, kept a wonderful diary of the war years, especially of the Blitz. She wrote of that night.

> Terrible fires in London, We went up on the roof to look. At Shepherd's Bush, flames were leaping, and towards the City they were gigantic. As I walked up the road I could see the smoke. A great red glow filled the sky – I had no need of a torch – I could see every step I took and could have read a book if I had wished. The police said it was Waterloo station, but a taxi man told my friend Miss Mowes that the City was on fire, and they were trying to save St Paul's. I shall never forget the horror of her first words to me.

At the *Daily Mail*'s office at Northcliffe House, Carmelite Street, Herbert Mason gazed on the inferno around St Paul's cathedral, a half mile away, and raised his camera. He later said:

> I focused at intervals as the great dome loomed up through the smoke. The glare of many fires and sweeping clouds of smoke kept hiding the shape. Then a wind sprang up. Suddenly, the

shining cross, dome and towers stood out like a symbol in the inferno. The scene was unbelievable. In that moment or two, I released my shutter.

Mason knew nothing of the drama at St Paul's, even as he took the picture that became the image of the Blitz. Falling rubble blocked emergency services getting through the streets and an abnormally low tide in the Thames caused hydrants on which firemen's pumps depended to run dry. When a fire broke out in the cathedral's library aisle, there was no mains water – the blaze was eventually stopped with stirrup pumps, buckets and sand.

Soon after 6.30pm, an incendiary bomb, one of twenty-nine to fall on St Paul's that night, pierced the lead roof of the dome and lodged in its timbers. Molten lead dripped into the nave below. The aged wood of the choir stalls and organ screen, carved by the great sculptor Grinling Gibbons, was at mortal risk, while smoke from the blazing buildings surrounding the cathedral enveloped it.

The American reporter Ed Murrow pronounced the great building's obituary in a live broadcast to the US. 'The Church that means most to London is gone. St Paul's Cathedral is burning to the ground as I talk to you now.' His valediction was premature. As he spoke, two specialist teams of firewatchers recruited from the Royal Institute of British Architects – and hand-picked because they had heads for heights – crawled along the wooden beams with hand pumps to reach the blazing section. But suddenly the incendiary bomb, having burnt through the wood, fell far, far to the nave below, where it was easily put out. Though almost every building around St Paul's perished, the cathedral survived.

More than 160 people died in that night's raid, including sixteen firemen, and 500 were injured. Eight of the firemen perished in a single incident when a wall collapsed on them as they fought a blaze near Fleet Street and 250 of their comrades suffered injuries during the night.

The morning was bitterly cold. There was light snow as office worker Dorothy Barton emerged from London Bridge station. She gazed in horror at the acres of smoking and still burning ruins. Then her heart lifted as she looked up at St Paul's towering over the scene. She said 'I felt a lump in my throat because, like so many people, I felt that while St Paul's survived so would we!' But mild, gentle Miss Vera Hodgson looked on the devastation and wrote bitterly, 'I shall never bother with Germans or foreigners again. It makes you want to give other people a taste of what we have had.'

Herbert Mason's photograph was not published for two days while censors considered whether it would serve Britain's cause. Other information about major damage and fatalities, such as at the Bank underground station during a raid, which killed 111 people sheltering on its platforms, was held up for as long as a year.

Mason, who was thirty-seven when he took his most famous shot, gave the original print to the landlord of *The Royal Bell*, Bromley, whose granddaughter Susan Campbell has it still. 'I've always been very proud of it,' she says. 'I'm really pleased that it's part of the nation's and the City's history.'

So it is! On New Year's Eve, two days after the raid, the censor gave his approval and the picture appeared in the *Daily Mail*, declared as 'One that all Britain will cherish, for it symbolises the steadiness of London's stand against the enemy, the firmness of Right against Wrong.'

The blitz on London continued for a further four months, until Hitler diverted the *Luftwaffe* to support his attack on Russia in May 1941, so the London Blitz ended. But in all, 43,000 people perished in air attacks on Britain, half of these in the capital. Britain's defiance against the Nazis had persisted, and the survival of the nation's greatest cathedral became its lasting symbol.

Bombing took its toll on London and disrupted the lives of its people. Roads and railways were damaged and destroyed along with other infrastructure such as sewers, and gas and water pipelines. Double-decker buses were blown into craters as if they had been thrown like a toy from an angry child's hand. At one point in time, the railway from Southampton terminated at Surbiton, twelve miles short of Waterloo. After the war a zone 100 yards wide was left flattened by bombs either side of the Southern Railway on the approach to London. In spite of all this, repairs to the city's infrastructure were carried out so quickly that German disruption of London's commerce and industry was mostly frustrated. The resilience of Londoners during the Blitz was legendary. Ordinary men, women and children showed amazing courage, carrying on with their daily lives in spite of the nightly bombing raids. In the end, many people were so used to them that they carried on with whatever they were doing. The Windmill theatre even put on its show with its slogan 'We never stopped'. Cinemas ran films during raids. And the audience stayed! The image of Londoners sheltering in Underground stations is a familiar one, but about 4 per cent of people used them. There was a terribly tragic accident at Bethnal Green underground station when a panic on an escalator caused the deaths of a hundred people at its base. But most Londoners stayed at home, preferring the warmth of their beds to the Anderson shelter's chill.

Knickebein
'The British will find what they are looking for, but they won't know they've got it!' laughed a captured German navigator. Between interrogations the aircrew were held in a room, but they did not know that it was bugged. The British wanted to find out how the German pathfinders' navigation was so accurate in finding their target. So after listening in, they checked every piece of gear on the crashed German aircraft, and concluded that it was the Lorenz landing system. They were right – this had been used internationally in military and civil aircraft since the mid-1930s, enabling pilots to land accurately at night or in bad weather. At the airfield two aerials each transmitted a wide beam. Their two beams overlapped on the centre line of the runway and carried Morse code, one dots, the other dashes. The spacing of the dots and dashes was fixed so that at the centre of the beams' overlap, the dots and dashes merged as a continuous tone known as the equi-signal, at the crossover between the two beams, a sharply accurate dividing line. This was far more accurate than the tedious and frustrating procedure of estimating the maximum signal at the centre of a single beam, so it

was a brilliant concept. When they used Lorenz in reverse and flew away from their airfield, it became Knickebein when another beam was transmitted, ideally at a right angle to the main beams, to cross at the British target. Obviously the original Lorenz equipment had to be upgraded, to remain accurate at ten times its usual range. Fast, accurate setting up of the two transmitter aerial groups was ensured by 100-foot aerials carried on circular tracks. Tight calibration ensured this extreme accuracy.

X-Gerät

After the British had defeated Knickebein, the Germans developed X-Gerät. Its name was well coded, as X marks a cross and X is also unknown! Knickebein had a problem – the bomber could transit the coded cross beam too quickly, but then have to correct this with a tight full turn. It could then return to its heading on the directional beam, but it would be safer for the aircraft missing the beam to abort its sortie, to avoid colliding with following bombers. X-Gerät avoided this problem with two prior warnings before the target. It used special equipment and four beams, the directional equi-signal beams and three cross beams. This made the transit across the final directional beam easier by using three transit points, visually rather than audibly. With its complexity it had to be used by the KGr 100 professional pathfinders, the ultimate group.

The directional beam was codenamed 'Weser'. The crossbeams 'Rhein', 'Oder' and 'Elbe' were transmitted from Cleves, just inside Germany. Each pathfinder, based at Vannes in Brittany, flew 150 miles after take-off to the 'Weser' transmitter near Cherbourg. The transmitted signal was similar to that on 'Knickebein', giving the aircraft easy acquisition of the beam, when the pilot would turn to port, and then fly northwards towards its British target accurately along the 'Weser' centreline given by its twenty feet wide equi-signal zone, until it was given the first warning by the 'Rhein' cross beam. From now on the pilot had to hold the 'Weser' centreline all the way to the target, ensured as both the pilot and the navigator had visual 'kicking' meters warning if the bomber strayed from the

31

centreline of the 'Weser' beam. The next cross beam, the 'Oder', was thirty kilometres from target, when the navigator had four seconds to respond. Here he started the system clock, when two hands, one green and one black, moved together for the next fifteen kilometres. Another hand, the red, remained stopped during this interval. Fifteen kilometres from the target the aircraft crossed the last beam, the 'Elbe', and the navigator stopped the green and black hands, which now gave him ground speed. This started the red hand on the clock moving towards its black hand. When the red and black hands coincided a circuit released flares over the target. X-Gerät was accurate to about 100 yards at 200 miles, close enough to hit a large factory when bomb ballistics and wind variations were fed in. It was the most accurate means of night bombing devised up to that time. It is hard to understand why the RAF could not destroy the 'Weser' directional beam transmitter near Cherbourg to prevent pathfinder guided raids. At that time the RAF was overstretched, and a raid on 'Weser' would have had lower strategic priority. But conversely X-Gerät damaged the British war effort more, razed a fine city and killed so many of its citizens. Both Knickebein and X-Gerät installations should have been obvious from the air, and their directional beams would have been obvious in an RAF attack. German operators would have had strict instructions to switch the gear off if an attack was coming their way. Thankfully the Germans did not install a transmitter on the Norwegian coast, similar to the one at Cherbourg. Then Cleves could have been useful for raids on the Tyne and Scotland as well, with an almost ideal 90° cut. But it is a sad irony that the German development has not since gone further in peacetime to prevent aircraft accidents such as that suffered by Air France flight AF 447. Radio navigation is very valuable, and gives pilots good secondary position and airspeed information if the primary pitot-static system fails.

The Coventry Blitz

X-Gerät was first used on the Coventry Blitz. On the moonlit night of 14 November 1940 the fine city of Coventry was destroyed, when over 500 German bombers made the biggest raid of the war on the heart of Britain's war production. Although the RAF used various aircraft to intercept German beams, and one or more of these may well have gone unserviceable that evening, there is no evidence that the loss contributed to the success of the German raid. These aircraft could only detect the beams and trace them to assess the position of the German target in Britain. In his memoirs *Most Secret War* Professor R.V. Jones proved that, at the time of the raid, the British had no effective countermeasures to the beams, and were not successful in blocking or 'bending' them. Later sources confirmed this. Countermeasures were used but these seemed to be ineffective. On the night of the raid on Coventry, British radio stations were transmitting on exactly the same frequencies as the beams, yet the Germans were able to follow their own transmissions and bomb Coventry anyway. But was this British inability to defend Coventry more deep-seated? Would the work of the Enigma code-breakers have been compromised to the point that many more British cities have been destroyed if we had countered that Blitz far more effectively? Why did Derby, very much the parallel city to Coventry, escape such ruination? Did the British succeed in distorting the beams over Derby after our monitor aircraft had found them?

In Edwardian times Coventry produced cycles and went on to make cars and planes, so the city was a major manufacturer, both in peace and war. Armstrong Whitworth, Daimler, Dunlop, GEC and Humber made everything there in the Second World War from bombers to scout cars. Most work was quickly transferred to shadow factories on the city outskirts, both to reduce the threat of aerial attack and also to remove it from residential areas.

Even before the Blitz, Coventry had been raided on 25 June 1940, when five bombs fell on Ansty Aerodrome. In October 1940 small raids left 176 dead. The RAF bombing of Munich, the birthplace of the Nazi Party on 8 November, gave the Germans an excuse to retaliate with Operation *Moonlight Sonata*, using KGr 100 pathfinders to start the raid on Coventry on 14 November 1940. At 7.00pm air raid sirens started and at 7.20pm the Bofors anti-aircraft guns fired at the planes overhead in the bright moonlit night. KGr 100 dropped white parachute flares on the city, followed by exploding phosphorus incendiary bombs, marking the target with fire to direct other bombers. Their bomb panniers opened at height to scatter incendiaries widely.

At 7.30pm the second group of planes started dropping the first of 500 tons of high explosives. Ordinary and exploding incendiaries fell with the bombs, which were nasty because you could extinguish an ordinary incendiary, only to be caught out by an exploding one. Some were aimed at industry around the city but most were concentrated on the city centre to create a firestorm. Early in the evening the Cathedral of St Michael was hit. By 7.40pm, despite their efforts, its defenders were defeated and the roof began to burn. By 8.00pm all fire engines in the city were fighting the flames. By dawn twenty-six firemen were dead and thirty-four seriously injured.

Many citizens hid in cellars, crypts and air raid shelters as the city was torn apart above them. Others stayed in their homes, thousands of which were either destroyed or damaged. The bombing continued, with the addition of terrible oil bombs and landmines. The mines drifted down on the end of a parachute, exploding just above ground level to smash everything under it. One destroyed the church of St Nicholas in Radford, leaving dead and injured in the crypt. Only one course of stones remained.

Even at 2.00am there was no let up, as the ground defences had run out of ammunition. Streets were levelled and factories blazed with the city centre. High explosive and incendiary bombs turned a hundred fires into one, as flames leapt 100 feet and the sky was just a smoky black cloak. Bombers 150 miles away could see the glow against the night. The Blitz ended at 6.15am as the all-clear sounded and slowly the shocked, frightened and tired people of Coventry emerged into what had once been their city.

The city wore a shroud of smoke and drizzle as dazed people wandered around taking in the destruction. In total, 4,330 homes were destroyed and three-quarters of the factories damaged. In this ruin some folk were never identified as 554 men, women and children lay dead and 865 were injured. It was miraculous that the figures were not higher as the city had been hit by 30,000 incendiaries, 500 tons of high explosive, fifty landmines and twenty oil bombs over eleven hours. The Germans were later put to shame as they used the word *Coventrate* in propaganda about this Blitz. This rebounded on the Germans as Coventry took the Soul of Mercy out of the British. As 'Bomber' Harris said 'They have sown the Wind – They shall reap the Whirlwind!' Berlin, Hamburg, Dresden and many other German cities were later hit very much harder as a result.

The tram system was destroyed, with tram lines ripped from the ground or arched into the air. Only seventy-three of the city's 181 buses remained. Practically all gas and water pipes were smashed and people were advised to boil supplies of water. Troops were drafted in by the hundreds to clear up the streets and the remains that littered them. Rescue parties, some specialists, others troops and the public, worked day and night trying to dig out the poor folk buried in the rubble of their homes. Ministry of Information vans toured the streets advising people where to get food and the homeless where to find shelter. Canteens were set up and within three days the Royal Engineers had restored electricity. Water and gas came on last.

Churchill visited the city, and the King toured the devastation on 16 November. On 20 November the first mass burial took place at the London Road Cemetery. Bodies continued to be recovered from the ruin of the city and in the following week a second mass burial took place. But smaller raids continued in the Easter week raids of 8 April and 10 April 1941, six and eight hours long. On 8 April Christchurch was burned out by incendiaries. The last bombing raid on Coventry was in August 1942. By then the city had suffered forty-one raids and 373 siren alerts. In total, 1,236 people were killed in the raids on Coventry, and 808 of these are buried in the mass grave in London Road Cemetery. Some had come to the city as war workers, and their families sadly collected them and took them home in plain wooden boxes. Some bodies were never identified. The raids changed Coventry for all time. Before the Blitz it had been described as the 'one of the finest preserved medieval cities in Europe'. The city centre's destruction accelerated plans that later introduced new architecture and Europe's first pedestrian precinct.

Luftwaffe raids on other towns

London and Coventry were by no means the only *Luftwaffe* targets. Some 236 bombers hit Clydebank, seven miles west of Glasgow, on 13 March 1941 and then came back the next night. They hit ship-yards, fuel tanks, and factories. The damage to the residential area was as heavy as it had been in the Warsaw Blitz at the start of the war. In total, 528 people died but local folk put this nearer 1,200. A landmine added to the tragic death-roll as it landed on a pub, killing those sheltering in its cellar; worse, they were cut to pieces so their last resting place had to be filled with quicklime. The Blitz was so secret that a soldier on surprise leave after the raids never saw his family but had to bury three of them.

There were two reasons for this major disaster. Sadly an RAF tactic of sandwiching bombers between ack-ack below and fighters above did not work, and was only tried this once. And as far as we know, the *Luftwaffe* pathfinder group, KGr 100, also made the obvious choice and took the lightly defended Irish Sea route, barely detected.

In the south, Portsmouth and Southampton were targets. Portsmouth was our premier naval base, and it was raided sixty-seven times when 40,000 bombs and mines were dropped on the city and dockyard, even damaging the Victory and its dry-dock. Its neighbour, Southampton, was home to the Vickers Supermarine factory and large docks. Belfast was also heavily raided on 15 April 1941, after 'Lord Haw-Haw', the traitor broadcaster, promised the raid.

Our seaside received surprise strikes after the German invasion of Russia, when the new Focke-Wulf FW190 fighter-bomber hit coastal towns. 'Lord Haw-Haw' did at least make Sussex folk laugh at his reference to the Worthing 'Gass-o-meters'. Then between April and June 1942 the *Luftwaffe* retaliated after RAF raids on similar German targets, and struck with the Baedeker raids (based on the Baedeker Guide) on Exeter (23/24 April) Bath (25/26 April), Norwich (27/29 April), York (28 April), and (after the bombing of Cologne) Canterbury (31 May, 2 and 6 June). The raids on these cities killed 1,637 civilians, injured 1,760, and destroyed over 50,000 houses. York's Guildhall and the Bath Assembly Rooms were damaged, but the cathedrals of Norwich, Exeter and Canterbury escaped. The German bombers suffered heavy losses in these raids.

Knowing what the Germans had done, we can understand how Watson-Watt was moved to beat them. The Germans had been hard on us, and now we would be tough on them in turn. The use of X-Gerät and other navigational aids 'makes your hair stand on end' – it does mine. There are people in that targeted town, who are either going to be dead or hideously injured in ten minutes. War is never pretty. But you have to remember the Latin motto *Si vis pacem, parere bellum* – If you want peace, prepare for war! We had to prepare for war by 1939, be ready to retaliate and outclass the Germans and win a just peace in 1945.

After the Battle of Britain the RAF fought less critical battles, ending the stalemate in the air and at sea. Thankfully, our AI ended the major Blitz in 1941

The British counter-strikes – ASV

The battle with the U-boats had to be won by the RAF and Navy in partnership, as no food or reinforcements would have otherwise reached us. A Sunderland fitted with ASV Mk 1 attacked a U-boat on 19 November 1940, and then a Whitley with ASV Mk 2 sank a U-boat on 10 February 1941. Navy success started 15 March 1941, and continuous ASV development improved the rate of U-boat sinking for both the RAF and Navy.

The Bruneval raid

The Combined Operations Raid on the German radar station at Bruneval, France, took place on the night of 27 February 1942.

The raid was initiated by R.V. Jones, who in 1939 was appointed as Britain's first Scientific Intelligence Officer. In 1941 he compared German radar with ours, by gathering information from German documents, crashed bombers and by interrogating POWs. Our approach to radar then was less sophisticated than that of the Germans in some ways, and more advanced in others. We used CH and AI. The Germans used the Freya reporting system comprising two complementary radars. The first was square, a large long-range, low-precision Freya, 25 feet high by 21 feet wide. The second was half its size, a short-range, high-precision Würzburg parabolic dish. The Germans were now adept in harmonizing the two, and brought down more British bombers. British losses made it necessary for us to identify these radars on site, using PR (Photo Reconnaissance) Spitfires. The distinctive Würzburg was first spotted in Holland, and then at coastal sites in France. If some new technique of ours could neutralize Würzburg the whole Freya system would be useless. So now Jones had to retrieve the essential parts of a Würzburg from a radar site. Of the coastal sites photographed, Bruneval was the easiest to attack!

Admiral Lord Mountbatten, the Combined Operations Commander, planned the raid. When he and his staff studied the radar site and its defence, he concluded it was too heavily guarded by local coastal defences to allow a commando raid. This would cost the commandos heavy casualties and not be fast enough to capture the Würzburg radar before the Germans destroyed it. Both surprise and speed were essential to capture the radar, so Mountbatten saw that an airborne assault was the only possible way. After some difficulties with readiness, 'C' Company of the 2nd Parachute Battalion was selected for the raid, commanded by Major John Frost. Wing Commander Pickard was chosen with his 51 Squadron to take them to Bruneval. The RAF finished their training and 'C' Company also successfully completed theirs, including instruction on the Bruneval layout. Now it was the Navy's turn to be brought in. During the training period, Major Frost was introduced to Commander Cook, Royal Australian Navy, who was to command the naval force evacuating the Company at the end of the raid, along with a party of thirty-two officers and men from 12 Commando to remain in the landing craft to cover the company as they withdrew from the beach at Bruneval. Frost also met the man for the operation, RAF Flight Sergeant Cox, who volunteered as an expert radio mechanic. It was Cox's job to locate and photograph the Würzburg radar, and dismantle it and bring it back to Britain. R.V. Jones tried to get Cox an Army uniform and number for the raid. If the raiders were captured Cox was the only one in Air Force uniform, therefore in danger of 'special attention' by the *Wehrmacht* and also the SS. Amazingly, the War Office, obdurate in its unimaginative thinking, refused. If the raid had failed it would have been responsible for his death and a major breach of security.

Information for the Bruneval radar was acquired during the training period by 'Remy' (Gilbert Renault) and his French resistance group. Their detailed knowledge of the German forces guarding the radar made the raid possible.

There were two parts to the radar installation. One hundred yards from the edge of a cliff a villa held the permanently manned Würzburg radar, surrounded by guard posts with thirty guards. Support buildings had a small garrison and technical personnel. In this enclosure there was a building holding a hundred troops, including another technical shift. An infantry platoon, stationed in Bruneval to the north, manned defences guarding the beach, which we needed for our evacuation. The defences included a strong point, pillboxes, and cliff top machine-gun nests overlooking the beach. This was not mined and had only patchy barbed-wire defence, but it was patrolled regularly. A mobile infantry reserve stationed some distance inland was also ready at an hour's notice. With this information, Frost split his men into five groups of forty men, each group given the name of an admiral, Nelson, Jellicoe, Hardy, Drake and Rodney. 'Nelson' would clear and hold the evacuation beach. 'Jellicoe', 'Hardy' and 'Drake' would capture the radar site and villa. 'Rodney', in reserve, would block the likely enemy approach in any counter-attack. The combination of full moon for visibility, and a rising tide for landing craft manoeuvres in shallow water, was vital for the success of the raid. This narrowed the dates to four days between 24 and 27 February.

So the planning was finished. A disastrous exercise on 23 February, when the landing craft grounded, forced a postponement of up to four days. But the weather was ideal on 27 February, so Commander Cook's naval force sailed in the afternoon, and the Whitley aircraft of 51 Squadron took off from RAF Thruxton with 'C' Company in the clear skies of evening. In spite of heavy ack-ack as they reached the French coast, not an aircraft was hit. They dropped 'C' Company at the correct point near the radar site, with the exception of half the Nelson group, which landed two miles short.

'Jellicoe', 'Hardy' and 'Drake' met no opposition as they surrounded the villa so Frost gave the order to open fire with grenades and automatics. They killed a German guard and took two prisoners, who said that most of the garrison were stationed inland. But the detachment in the enclosure next to the villa opened fire on the airborne troops, killing one of them. German fire increased and enemy trucks were seen moving out of the woods towards the villa. It worried Frost even more that his radio sets did not work as he could not talk to other detachments, especially to 'Nelson' who had to clear the beach. He was happy when Flight Sergeant Cox and his sappers arrived and dismantled the radar equipment. Once they had finished Frost ordered a withdrawal to the beach, which unknown to him had not then been secured, made obvious when a Company Sergeant Major was severely wounded by machine gun fire. Frost ordered 'Rodney' and part of 'Nelson' to clear the beach, and took the rest of 'C' Company back to the villa after clearing it again of enemy troops. When he returned to the beach, he found the other part of 'Nelson' had reached the beach, and attacked and cleared the machine-gun nest. At 02.15 hours, no naval force had shown up, so Frost ordered 'Nelson' to guard the inland approaches to the beach. He then fired a signal flare seawards, and was relieved to see the naval force coming in. There was confusion as the landing craft evacuated 'C' Company, the two POWs, and Flight Sergeant Cox's technical group with the captured radar gear from the beach. Once out to sea, everyone was transferred to motor gun boats, finishing their eventful task with an escort of four destroyers and a flight of Spitfires.

Flight Sergeant Cox must have felt proud!

The success of the Bruneval raid had four major effects. It lifted British morale as it was a major successful raid on France, even if reports deliberately omitted the reasons for it. Churchill and the War Cabinet were given full details by Frost and the other leaders.

All the major figures including Frost were awarded medals, Cox the Military Medal; on 15 May the *London Gazette* announced the award of nineteen decorations.

The War Office also followed up with the establishment of the Airborne Forces Depot and Battle School, and created the Parachute Regiment.

Examination of the Würzburg radar helped us in several ways. Its modular design helped maintenance, making fault-finding much simpler than on British equivalents. Previously, it had been proof against conventional jamming, but this newly complete knowledge of the Würzburg's working frequency paved the way for Window, the simple passive jammer that reduced our bomber losses then and later, so the raid was both successful and completely relevant.

The raid also showed the vulnerability of the TRE (Telecommunications Research Establishment) at Swanage, Dorset. So it was moved to Malvern School, to become the real 'School for Secrets' in Worcestershire, so well portrayed in Peter Ustinov's first documentary film, with a memorable portrayal by John Laurie. In its own distinctive way it also referred to the sad loss of Blumlein in an aircraft accident.

Its move to Malvern was so secret that it apparently lost quite a few of its personnel on the way. Just imagine coming back from leave to find the place had disappeared!

GEE

Daily, people in Lübeck see the Marienkirche bells, half broken, and half melted at the base of the bell tower; their postcards recall that blitz. Berlin, Cologne and Dresden grieve about the dreadful destruction of their cities during the war, but they have to remember that German airmen smashed Warsaw, London and Coventry before this!

War seen by the innocents on either side is awful, but bomb aimers can't appreciate what they have unleashed, because what they see below is remote, a mile below them. Yes, the Germans had hit us hard, striking most of our cities terribly, but now they were going to suffer far worse counter-strikes, enabled by our new developments.

The first to swing the air battle our way was GEE. RAF night navigation accuracy improved far beyond that of dead reckoning when this new gear made sorties more efficient as our bombs hit the target instead of the German countryside. R.J. Dippy proposed the concept in October 1937, but deferred it in view of other priorities. In spite of its codename GEE (for Grid), its charts overlaid its maps with hyperbolic lines. This title must have wasted some *Luftwaffe* code-breaker's time, as he looked with great frustration for some neat square grid. Instead hyperbolic charts were generated by four coded pulsed transmitters in Britain, a master and three phase-locked slaves. The system resembled a starburst with the master at the centre and three individually coded slaves eighty miles away, at equilateral points. The system gave three straight lines in the hyperbolic set, each one at the equi-phase line, the centreline between the master and each slave. CRTs contributed greatly to GEE as a primitive graticule fixed to the tube face improved the accuracy of its electronic measurement and in other gear later on. GEE was an improvement on Knickebein and X-Gerät as it needed no mechanical resetting of the transmitters. Like Decca Navigator it required no transmissions from aircraft using it, so German fighters could not home on GEE in our aircraft. They took five months to apply counter-measures instead of the three anticipated by the RAF, and this was due to tight security, both within the RAF and its suppliers. The range for GEE was about 350 miles, but could exceed 700 miles on some sorties over Italy. It accurately marshalled a bomber fleet, and held it on track all the way to the target, which it hit as a cohesive force. It left no stragglers at the mercy of German fighters, and helped to bring damaged aircraft back to the nearest airbase. If the target was beyond GEE range, then dead reckoning improved as it only needed to start at the GEE limit. This was the case for early use of GEE for the raids by 300 bombers on the neighbouring towns of Lübeck and Rostock on 8 and 9 March 1942. Later, again in March, 120 bombers used GEE at a much shorter range to bomb Cologne in a raid lasting only fifteen minutes, and they all kept to their schedule for return to base to within two minutes. It was Cologne's turn again on 31 May 1942, this time for a thousand bomber raid, when the bombers overwhelmed the German defence; no wonder most of Cologne was flattened by the end of the war. Three other GEE installations were set up, firstly covering Brest, Lorient and St Nazaire. Coastal Command used the second and third over the Atlantic.

Oboe

Hermann Goering himself famously praised the brilliant de Havilland Mosquito bomber, the pathfinder bomber that used Oboe against the Germans.

> In 1940 I could at least fly as far as Glasgow in most of my aircraft, but not now! It makes me furious when I see the Mosquito. I turn green and yellow with envy. The British, who can afford aluminium better than we can, knock together a beautiful wooden aircraft that every piano factory over there is building, and they give it a speed which they have now increased yet again. What do you make of that? There is nothing the British do not have. They have the geniuses and we have the nincompoops. After the war is over I'm going to buy a British radio set – then at least I'll own something that has always worked.

A.H. Reeves developed this, the war's most accurate navaid. Oboe used two well separated home stations, giving a cut near the 90° ideal. Both transmitted individually coded signals to a radio transponder in the Mosquito pathfinder, which returned the signals to the two stations. The signal's return time (10.74μ-seconds/mile) gave the distance to the aircraft from each station. Oboe's high accuracy was compromised by less accurate Ordinance Survey detail across the Channel, so Belgian Resistance were given prior details of the target for the first Oboe raid, on the German night-fighter HQ at Florennes in southern Belgium they had reported. They were asked again, this time for distance between aiming points and hits. It was accurate to yards, and Oboe proved to be the best Second World War navigational aid, as the HQ building received a direct hit. Also,

43

the Belgian Resistance were gratified with our thanks for their commitment and high standards!

Each Oboe station used radio ranging to give a pre-arranged circle's radius, and two circles intersected to pinpoint the target. The aircraft flew along the circumference of the circle defined by the 'Cat' station, and dropped its load of flares or bombs when, with a prior code, it reached the intersection with the other circle given by the 'Mouse' station. The circular path defined by the 'Cat' was at a slightly smaller radius to compensate for the different flights, straight for the bombs after release and circular for the aircraft. There was a network of Oboe stations in the south of England, and any station could be operated as Cat or Mouse as needed. Mk 1 Oboe was developed from Chain Home Low concepts, operating at 1.5 metres or 200 MHz. The two stations emitted a series of pulses at about 133 times per second. The pulse width could be made short or long so that it was received by the aircraft as a Morse code dot or dash. The 'Cat' station sent dots if the aircraft was inside the needed radius and dashes if it was outside. The pilot kept his course using this. It was vulnerable to jamming and detection of its aircraft. But that needed methodical logging by the Germans and they took eighteen months, much longer than the RAF planners had allowed, because pathfinders used the fast Mosquito. So the RAF went for the most important target, the armaments centre at Essen. In the first raid on 21 December 1942, 50 per cent of the bombs hit the target, later improving to a consistent 50 per cent success rate of 45 yards, when bombing from 6,000 feet. On 15 March 1943, 400 RAF bombers systematically started destroying the Ruhr, forcing the Germans to repair the Ruhr installations using 50,000 labourers from the construction of the Atlantic Wall fortifying the Dutch, Belgian and French coasts. Some 627 aircraft dropped 2,000 tons of bombs on Essen in the final raids on 25 and 26 July 1943, and completely stopped Krupp armament production, so matching the impact on Coventry. In total, 1,500 homes were destroyed in Essen and 1,100 badly damaged. Most of the Krupp works were destroyed, killing 340 and injuring 1,130, a sad result of a justifiable raid.

H2S

H2S combined the HF cavity magnetron and the CRT. (This 50 GHz microwave device generates a pulse power of megawatts. At its centre a cathode emits electrons that oscillate in and near resonant cavities cut in a copper block. The electrons leave at an output loop anode in one of the cavities.) It gave bombers a video map for raids on the Ruhr, Cologne, Hamburg and other German cities, industrial areas such as Essen, and military installations such as Peenemünde. H2S identified ground targets for night and all-weather bombing, using the different reflectivity of water, ground, and buildings, to show them up as a map. You could see Hamburg with its dockyards on the Elbe, the city itself and its surrounding countryside. The earliest equipments were known as TR3159 (H2S Mk I and ASV VIB) and TR3191 (H2S Mk II).

On 30 January 1943, H2S was used in RAF bomber navigation for the first time, and it was the first ground mapping radar used for combat. Stirling and Halifax pathfinder bombers now had an accurate map for navigation and night bombing, *and* it did not need a degree in mathematics to use it.

H2S used ten-centimetre radar of 9.1cm wavelength. Its design was possible due to the development of cavity magnetron. Later versions cut wavelength to 3cm and then 1.5cm, when it could detect rain clouds. The cavity magnetron had one operational weakness. It was indestructible, and its use would be very obvious to any German scientist after its recovery from a crashed RAF bomber. The RAF understood this weakness well before operational use. In trials they tried to smash it, but it was so robust that it remained almost unscathed after a ten foot hole had been blown in the test fuselage. It was a pity they couldn't add some friable material to the magnetic mix, but H2S was urgently needed and this would have delayed development. On a Cologne raid in February 1943, a Stirling pathfinder was shot down over Rotterdam on its second operational use. The Germans named H2S the Rotterdam Gerät after the crash site. The electronics firm Telefunken repaired and rebuilt the damaged H2S set except for the smashed CRT. This led to the development of the Naxos radar detector, homing *Luftwaffe* fighters on to H2S transmissions. This made the RAF pathfinders using H2S vulnerable to the German counterstroke, which was a pity because it was so brilliant.

Window – passive jamming

The simplest jamming is passive, but no less effective for that. You can blind enemy radar with half wavelength aluminium foil strips. Both sides knew this, so they were frightened to use it or even to breathe a word about it, almost like 'You must never mention her name in the Mess', to quote a later well known comic song by the Goons. Watson-Watt had used a balloon carrying a wire of critical length for gun-laying tests in 1937, and its radar return was so obvious that the gun crew could 'see' it twenty-five miles away. To stop the Germans following this up with new developments, he forbade its use when wind could have carried it to the continent. British tactics were to maintain secrecy for the development of 'Window', its British codename. The common German radar was the 'Würzburg' parabolic dish. This 560MHz radar's wavelength was 53.5 centimetres and its half wavelength 10.5 inches. Its transmitter frequency and wavelength would have to be changed radically if the British could blind it. German dependence on Würzburg would give the British several months of unhindered air strikes, and so the RAF held Window in reserve to bring it out at the most suitable and critical time. A test drop of Window festooned much of Britain, an event I well remember, and this was followed on 24 July 1943 by our raid on Hamburg. The fury between German fighter pilots and their controllers must have exploded. As a pilot, you are directed to a location to find nothing, and not just once but time after time – and your AI radar is totally useless. As a controller all you see is a fog of ghostly doppelgangers on your radar screens, slowly drifting down through the sky like a snowstorm. All you can do is scream 'Doppel'. Above them, British aircrew are busy tearing Window packets open with funny looks, and throwing them out the door with parting shots like, 'This is magic!'

The British could reconfigure their radar to counter a similar German counter-strike, but such raids need time to set up, even with the reduced German bomber force. Hamburg then suffered an American daylight raid and another night raid by the RAF, when the docks and inner city area were almost burnt out. In the ensuing months our bomber losses halved, and never returned to the level before Window. It also featured later in D-Day deception, when the RAF dropped Window in a synchronized pattern on the approach to the Pas de Calais, to simulate a large invasion fleet

Active jamming

Watson-Watt saw how an enemy could nullify CH radar echoes by transmitting another beam on a similar frequency. Active jamming is only effective if the power is sufficient, but our power level could not counter the X-Gerät transmission at the time of the Coventry raid. Other techniques modulated the beam so that returning echoes on display were unreadable. Jamming was not underestimated so Dr R. Cockburn was appointed head of a Radio Countermeasures Unit, which built a jammer – 'Aspirin'. This transmitter masked German transmissions at the Cherbourg installation. The RAF set up 'J-Watch' to monitor and record 'jamming' transmissions, to record their frequencies, and to pinpoint the source. It monitored frequencies from 20MHz to 3,000MHz.

J-Watch used several devices:

Code	Description of jamming device
IFRU	Two tunable filters in the receiver minimize continuous-wave interference
IJAJ	A special circuit suppressing pulsed interference
AJBO	A special circuit suppressing frequency-modulated interference

Decca navigator

Watson-Watt was offered this hyperbolic system in 1939. He rejected it then as it was vulnerable to jamming, but Allied ships used it later on D-Day. Its four stations, Master, Red, Green, and

Purple Slaves, transmitted continuous RF carrier, the main radio frequency carrying the lower information frequencies. The Master was at the centre of three slaves set at equi-angular positions. Each slave transmitted unmodulated phase stable carrier waves, harmonics of a common 14.2kHz reference frequency 'f', with slave reference oscillators phase locked to the '6f' Master shown. Phase comparisons of the synchronized transmissions gave the chart position, shown on three 'Deccometers', coded Red, Green and Purple.

Decca system requirements

Master or slave	Slave colour	Frequency multiplier	Band
Master		6f	in the 85 kHz band
Slave	Red	8f	in the 112 kHz band
Slave	Green	9f	in the 127 kHz band
Slave	Purple	5f	in the 71 kHz band

The device proved so accurate that it was used as a test reference for post Second World War equipment such as TACAN, the range and bearing navaid.

A summary of Robert Watson-Watt's work

Without radar and its developments, along with those of the Merlin, Spitfire and Hurricane, we would have been defeated in the Battle of Britain and over-run by the *Luftwaffe*. The Germans would have obliterated our cities and our Armed Services, as we readied our-selves to meet invasion. Watson-Watt gave us a level playing-field with that all-seeing eye, and stopped German attempts to crush Britain. He gave us our freedom with the equipment for the war on all fronts, ultimately to counter their horrendous V-weapons, and attain final victory.

A German air marshal, Adolf Galland, remarked at the end of the War 'In battle we had to rely on our eyes; the British pilots could rely on radar which was far more reliable and had a longer range. Our briefings were three hours old; the British were virtually instantaneous.' Germans, such as Galland, could be generous even in defeat.

His British opponent, Dowding, commented 'Where would we have been without radar? We could never have maintained the vast number of standing patrols that would have been necessary without that magic eye.'

Watson-Watt's ethos permeated the British war effort, as his work on radar reached every similar offensive and defensive weapon. From industry's start Scots like Robert Watson-Watt have included brilliant inventors and engineers, coloured with offbeat but delightfully intelligent humour, as I know well. He showed it when a radar-gun toting policeman pulled him over in Canada for speeding, with 'Had I known what you were going to do with it I would never have invented it!' He wrote the following poem:

Rough Justice

Pity Sir Robert Watson-Watt, strange target of this radar plot
And thus, with others I can mention the victim of his own invention.
His magical all-seeing eye enabled cloud-bound planes to fly,
But now by some ironic twist it spots the speeding motorist
And bites, no doubt with legal wit, the hand that once created it.

His contribution to the war effort was rewarded with a knighthood in 1942. In 1952 the British Government awarded him £50,000 for his work on radar development. But his marriage to Margaret didn't survive the war, and in 1952 he married his second wife, Jean, who was more attuned to his wanderlust than Margaret, who wanted to stay in Scotland. Increasingly despondent about the lack of further acknowledgement of his achievements, Sir Robert moved to Canada where he spent much of the post-war era.

Jean seems to have disappeared off his radar by 1966. At the age of seventy-two he married Kathryn Trefusis Forbes, the founding Air Commander of the WAAF operations arm of RAF radar. He survived her death in 1971, and died on 5 December 1973. Both are buried in the churchyard of the Episcopal Church of the Holy Trinity at Pitlochry.

Was Sir Robert Watson-Watt justified to have that 'guid' conceit o' himsel'?

To answer, he started out in relatively simple physics, and then went on to develop radar, different from the Germans', but one that worked *and* kept them at bay.

And he created an ethos in which so many new developments came to birth.

Yes, he was radar's pivotal figure!

Notes on CH system p.r.f. and range

The CH designer allowed for the large fly-back time of primitive CRTs, so:

1. Let p.r.f. = 400Hz, conveniently one of the usual RAF equipment frequencies.
2. Allow for a 2 per cent tolerance, lifting this frequency to 408Hz.
3. Maximum periodic time for system = 1/408 = 2,450.9µ seconds.
3. CRT fly-back time and other delays will reduce this by say 50µ seconds.
4. System running time remaining = 2,401µ seconds.
5. Out and back time per mile = 10.74µ seconds.
6. Possible maximum range is 2,401/10.74 = 223.55 statute miles.
7. Therefore typical maximum range that can be set = 220 statute miles.

Chapter 2

Frederick Henry Royce and the Merlin

Henry Royce, as he preferred to be called, was born the fifth child of a miller, on 27 March 1863 in Huntingdonshire. The mill was unusual in that it was both steam and water powered; it was from the millrace that Henry was saved at the age of two whilst inspecting the millwheel. At the age of four he was earning money for bird scaring and as the mill failed suffered from poverty and a meagre diet, conditions that were to be his lot until his teenage years. The mortgage on the mill was foreclosed and Henry and his elder brother were taken to London by their father, leaving the rest of the family in the local poor house.

Henry sold newspapers and only attended school for one year. He became a telegraph boy, his area being Mayfair. It was in this area that Charles Stewart Rolls was born on 22 August 1877; did Henry deliver the congratulatory telegrams to his parents? On holiday in 1877 with his aunt in Peterborough, Henry discussed his concern about his future prospects. His aunt offered to pay the £20 annual premium for him to start an apprenticeship at the Great Northern Railway (GNR) works in Peterborough. This was the first of many examples of the fortunate occurrences that would help him during his lifetime.

Henry was boarded with a GNR employee, Mr Yarrow, who had a fully equipped workshop in his garden. Here in the evenings he honed his skills in fitting, filing and machining. He also tried to use

51

any spare time to improve his education. However, after three years he had to leave GNR as his aunt could no longer afford to pay the premium. He walked from Peterborough to Leeds (118 miles!) where he found a job as a toolmaker. At that time his mother was living in Leeds with one of his sisters. In 1881, reading about the new-fangled electricity, he returned to London to join the Electric Light and Power Company. Here he managed to further his education by attending evening classes at the London Polytechnic. His progress with the company was such that in 1882, at the age of nineteen, he was posted to Liverpool as a chief electrician installing theatre and street electric lighting. However, in 1883 the company had folded.

Henry and his friend Ernest Claremont decided to start up a business manufacturing small electrical components; Henry had £20 and Ernest £50, probably borrowed from his father. He came from a very different 'middle class' background to Henry, and one wonders how they came together. Claremont, the son of a London doctor, was privately educated and at University College London. He then trained at the Brush Electrical Engineering Company; during this time it is possible that he met Henry Edmunds, who would later play a major role in the fortunes of the Royce Company.

So in 1884 the two young men moved to Cook Street in Manchester. The company was titled F.H. Royce & Co., Electrical and Mechanical Engineers. Henry was a year older than Ernest and that might explain why the latter did not get a mention in the title of the company; he was however, listed as a partner.

Their first products were filaments for light bulbs and switches, Henry designing and making the tooling and fixtures. Claremont handled orders and finances. Their initial workforce consisted of four girls. Henry and Ernest lived frugally above the workshop and their favourite recreation seemed to be a card game called grab. Henry embarked on his lifetime habit of long hours of work and neglect of food, which would later have serious effects on his health. Ernest, on the other hand, was quite athletic; amongst his interests was wrestling. Initially it was a struggle to make ends meet, but some slight financial alleviation came with the introduction of a door bell set that sold well.

The major breakthrough came with Henry's invention of a spark-less commutation dynamo. Its application, particularly in hazardous areas, resulted in an increase in the workforce and an increase in the factory area.

A further product introduced at this time was a tram motor controller. The financial situation was aided to a large extent by contracts from the Manchester Ship Canal Company.

In 1893 Henry married Minnie Punt, whose sister had married Ernest Claremont the previous year. Minnie brought with her a considerable dowry of £1,500 and although there is little mention of her thereafter, he did build a house in Knutsford and their entwined initials were placed above the front door. Typically, he installed lighting in the garden to enable him to work after dark. It seemed that Henry was very content with life at this stage, contemporary reports remark on his habit of smoking a pipe and singing Gilbert and Sullivan songs when in good humour (he had a fine tenor voice) but it was also reported that he could swear pretty well when annoyed.

In 1894 Henry turned his attention to crane construction. These became renowned for reliability, and particularly in foundry use with his design, which eliminated spillage when stopping or starting the transfer of molten metal. One of these cranes was still in working order in 2002 situated in an ex-marine engine facility on Clydeside, Glasgow. He also designed an improved tram controller unit.

The company went from strength to strength with orders increasing from £6,000 in 1897 to £20,000 in 1899. In that year the company was floated on the stock market as Royce Ltd and work started on a new factory, designed by Henry, in Manchester. The factory opened in 1901 with another significant figure, Henry Edmunds, as a major shareholder, who would have a profound influence on the company later. Edmunds trained as an engineer, showing early promise by taking a patent on ideas for improvements to heating and lighting at the age of twenty in 1874. He soon became interested in electricity and this continued for many years, on one occasion taking him to the USA to meet with Thomas Edison. His working life brought him into contact with many pioneers in such developments as phonographs, incandescent lighting, telephones and engines. During this time he invested in and was on the board of many companies. He became heavily involved with Joseph Swan in the development of the incandescent lamp. In 1897 he was elected a member of the Royal Institution.

Quite naturally he became interested in the appearance of the first motor cars and in 1898 he bought a De Dion motor tricycle, eventually graduating to a Daimler car and joining the Royal Automobile Club. In 1900 he entered the 1,000 miles trial in which he won a bronze medal in his class, and importantly met Charles Rolls, the start of a long friendship that would prove mutually beneficial. In 1901 Edmunds became a partner in WT Glover, an electrical and telephone cable company. Their premises were opposite the Royce Factory in Trafford Park, and in due course Edmunds made the acquaintance of Royce, a chain of connections between influential people that we shall see repeated later.

Shortly after the flotation of the company a major recession occurred, coupled with the advent of cheaper American cranes on the market. The Board wanted to reduce the quality of the Royce cranes to match the competition. Henry refused as he was convinced that there remained a market for quality equipment.

Concerned with Henry's continued neglect of his health, Claremont bought him a French De Dion car as a distraction. This car was dismissed with the comment 'It's just two bicycles joined by an engine'. At this time the long hours of work and poor eating habits led to Henry collapsing. Minnie put her foot down and persuaded him to accompany her on a ten-week cruise to South Africa. On his return he purchased a French Decauville car, which he dismantled, and to the dismay of the Board members, at a time of continued recession, declared he would build a better car.

In 1904 the first Royce car, with a two-cylinder engine, was produced and immediately started on an intensive development test programme. As parts failed they were examined and redesigned by Henry. The result of this continuous 'test and improve' approach, which was Henry's way of working throughout his career, was a reliable and remarkably quiet machine. Claremont was tasked with driving a car as part of this programme; he had a notice on the dash which read 'If this car breaks down do not ask any foolish questions', and he also took the precaution of having a horse and carriage on hand!

The Hon. Charles Rolls, who sold cars to the aristocracy, was seeking a British car of quality. He was advised by Henry Edmunds that Henry Royce had produced an impressive car. Charles was not interested in a two-cylinder car and Henry was too busy to travel to London. However, after arbitration by Henry Edmunds, Charles was persuaded to visit Henry. They met in Manchester on 4 May 1904, and there was an instant rapport between Henry, aged forty-one, and Charles, aged twenty-seven. Having had a demonstration of the 10hp two-cylinder car, Charles was so impressed that he ordered nineteen two-cylinder and six three-cylinder models. It was agreed that that these cars would be known as Rolls-Royce and this was formalized in 1906 with the formation of the Rolls-Royce Company.

Charles Rolls, the son of Lord and Lady Llangattock, was born in London in 1877. In 1891 he followed his elder brothers to Eton. Whilst there, he showed an aptitude for engineering by installing a dynamo in the Welsh home of the family for partial electric lighting, and experimenting with the estate steamroller when his parents were absent. He was accepted as a candidate for the Grenadier Guards but, fortunately, it was decided he would be placed with a private crammer as a prelude to university. This was effective in that it included his attendance at lectures by a Professor of Applied Mechanics, resulting in him gaining an entrance to Trinity College Cambridge to study engineering. His studies at Cambridge were interrupted by his purchase of a Peugeot car in Paris, followed by Bolée and De Dion motor tricycles (in the latter case the same machine as Royce and Edmunds used) and his involvement in cycle racing, becoming captain of the university team in 1897. He graduated in 1898 with a Class 2 ordinary Bachelor of Arts Degree 'by Special examination in Mechanism and Applied Science' and he had been accepted as a student member of the Institution of Civil Engineers. After a short spell as Third Engineer on the family steam yacht, he then worked, briefly; in the workshops of the London and North Western Railway in Crewe.

He became involved in driving in the early car races with some successes, but he also took up the sport of ballooning in 1901, continuing until shortly before his death in 1910, winning awards in the 1906 Gordon Bennett event with third place and the longest duration flight with his own Britannia balloon. As he would later with aircraft, he campaigned with the military for recognition of the balloon for warfare. He still found time to win the 1906 Isle of Man Tourist Trophy with a four-cylinder Rolls-Royce engine.

Due to the increased volume of work it became necessary to build a new factory; the choice of the site in Derby was influenced by the low electricity costs. The factory was designed by Henry on similar lines to his Manchester factory. This was retained as part of the Royce Ltd Crane Company, which would continue to conduct business until 1931. Many members of the Manchester workforce moved to the Derby factory by their own means, in some cases by walking. The new factory was officially opened by Lord Montague in July 1908. Henry continued to design new cars including four- and six-cylinder models; these latter cars featured the famous radiator design that resulted from the need for improved cooling. In the autumn of 1906 Henry produced what was to become 'the best car in the world', an improved 7.5-litre six-cylinder car, later christened the Silver Ghost by Claude Johnson, a marketing genius. He had joined the company at the same time as Rolls and was to be yet another of the people who had a tremendous effect on the prosperity of the company.

The son of a glover, Claude was born in 1864. Possibly as the result of gaining a scholarship, he was educated at the expensive St Paul's private school. On finishing school he enrolled in the Royal College of Art. He soon realized that a career in the world of art was not for him and at the age of nineteen he became a clerk at the Imperial Institute. Due to his innate ability for marketing and publicity he soon began to organize exhibitions at the Institute. In 1886 the Prince of Wales decided to hold a motor vehicle exhibition at the Imperial Institute and requested that Claude should be in charge of the organization. The success of this exhibition brought Claude's name to the attention of major figures in the automobile industry and would lead to his appointment as the Secretary to the fledgling Royal Automobile Club (RAC). It was here that he met one of the founders of the RAC, Charles Rolls. During his time with the RAC Claude was the driving force behind its rapid growth; amongst his many achievements were the introduction of the 'triptych' form that he had agreed with foreign countries and would simplify Customs formalities for motorists; vetting and licensing hotels; the touring department; engineering department; and diamond-shaped green and white boards at danger spots on the roads. In addition, he organized the 1,000-mile trial in which both Rolls and Edmunds competed; small wonder that his annual salary reached £1,000.

In 1903 he decided a change of occupation was required. He joined the Automobile Sales organization of C.S. Rolls & Co. It should be noted that Claude was an impressive figure, over six feet tall and always immaculately dressed. With his contacts and organizing skills he was a very welcome addition to this burgeoning company. He became commercial director of Rolls-Royce on the formation of the company in 1906.

He immediately started a campaign of spectacular events. His great marketing successes were to enter the Silver Ghost in the Scottish six-day trial in 1907 and for the car to go on to set a new record of 15,000 miles without an unscheduled stop, beating the existing Napier record of 7,000 miles. Other successes included the Spanish Grand Prix and a 1, 2, 3, 4 finish in the Alpine trials. At this time he was responsible for ensuring that the Board agreed that car production was limited to the Silver Ghost.

In 1908 another man who was to have a long-lasting influence on the future of the company arrived at Derby railway station. Emerging into a rain-swept dreary Midland road, Ernest Hives tossed a coin to decide if he should bother to attend the job interview at Rolls-Royce; fortunately it came down the right way.

Hives was born in 1886 in Berkshire; in 1899 he started a three-year apprenticeship with an engineering company in Reading. It happened that this company was also involved with cars and he spent evenings learning all he could about the mechanics of these fascinating machines. He learned to drive by moving cars in the garage, to such good effect that he took to the open road at the age of fourteen, teaching a lady to drive. In 1903 he met Charles Rolls whom he helped when he had a problem with his car. This resulted in Hives becoming Rolls' chauffeur and for a short time he worked at the Rolls Company. This was followed by employment at the Napier factory where he drove one of their cars in the 1906 and 1907 Scottish Trials where he would have seen the Silver Ghost. He drove a Napier at the second meeting at the new Brooklands race track. When he joined Rolls-Royce in 1908 he was appointed as an experimental tester. He soon made his name in endurance testing in all weather conditions. He was chosen to drive the Silver Ghost in the 1911 London to Edinburgh non-stop run in top gear. Later that year he lapped Brooklands at 101mph in a modified Silver Ghost.

He demonstrated his engineering skill with a chassis bump rig (standard equipment at car manufacturers these days). This led to a cure for stub axle failures. In 1912, with Royce now based in the winter months at La Canadel, Hives realized this provided an opportunity for extended endurance testing in France, clocking up 10,000 miles in a 40/50 model. Hives at times drove the courier service between Derby and West Wittering carrying drawings, memos etc., to and from Royce. He took pride in having set the record time for the journey. There is no doubt that Royce formed a high opinion of his technical aptitude and his leadership, demonstrated when he was team leader during the successful win in the 1913 Alpine Trial.

With the outbreak of war in 1914 he was involved in the development of the armoured car and then, as we shall see later, in the Eagle and subsequent aero engines.

What a loss for Rolls-Royce on that rainy day in 1908, if the coin had come down the other way!

In the meantime Charles Rolls had met the Wright brothers and his enthusiasm was such that he immediately purchased a Wright glider for basic flying experience and then graduated to powered fight in October 1909. He had quite a struggle to master the French-built Wright Flyer, suffering a number of accidents. However he rapidly became so proficient that he was selected to instruct pilots of the fledgling Military Air Arm. He was the second person to receive a pilot's certificate from the Aero Club of Great Britain. He found the control loads tiring and persuaded Orville Wright that the addition of a tailplane would help resolve the problem, which he was convinced was due to an incorrect centre of gravity. This was successful and Rolls continued to analyse the design of the Wright, passing on criticisms and suggestions to the Wright brothers. In all, he purchased six Wright aircraft. On 2 June 1910 he made the first non-stop two-way crossing of the English Channel, completing the trip with a pass over the Blériot memorial by Dover Castle.

Charles continued to take every opportunity to foster the importance of aircraft for the military and to enter various flying competitions. For the Bournemouth Aviation Meeting, which was to run from 11 to 16 June 1910, he fitted a moving tailplane to improve pitch control. On 12 June, whilst taking part in a spot landing competition in windy conditions, he made a steep approach and when levelling out the tailplane failed. The aircraft dived vertically from 80 feet and Charles Rolls was killed.

We can only guess at what his contribution to aviation might have been and how his future involvement with the company would have developed. Charles, having failed to persuade Henry there was a future in aviation, had been planning to embark on aircraft production.

Claude Johnson continued to pursue every opportunity to publicize the Silver Ghost. A typical effort was the attempt on the stop and restart test at Jasper Hill (the steepest accessible road at that time), which defeated many cars. Claude loaded the Silver Ghost with nine stout men and the stop and restart was completed with ease. The demand for the Silver Ghost exceeded production capability, resulting in the wait for delivery that would remain a feature of the car division for many years.

In 1911 Claude contacted Charles Sykes, who had provided illustrations for the car brochures, and asked him to design a mascot for the car radiators. Modelled by Eleanor Thornton who was secretary to

Lord Montague, the resultant 'Spirit of Ecstasy' raised some eyebrows at the time but has remained on Rolls-Royce cars, with some small changes, through the years. It is presumed that Claude organized the competition that resulted in the famous interlinked 'R's being the winning design, by a Beatrice Eccles.

In 1911 Henry was again taken seriously ill, to the extent that the doctors only gave him three months to live. While he was convalescing, Claude Johnson, who was deeply concerned that the loss of this man, would have a disastrous effect on the future of the company delegated his duties in order to resolve this problem. To the amazement of the doctors Henry overcame his illness by sheer willpower. Claude then took him on an extended tour across France and Italy in a Silver Ghost, spending the winter in Egypt. In the spring of 1912, motoring along the south coast of France, they stopped to admire the view at the small village of La Canadel. Claude was surprised when Henry stated he would like to build a house there. Claude immediately got to work for here was an opportunity to get him away from the factory in Derby, where he got involved in just about everything that was going on, and continued his habit of working late at night. Henry could not stand what he regarded as maltreatment of machines such as taking, in his opinion, too large a cut when turning parts on a lathe. He would sack the offender on the spot only for Claude to meet the 'miscreant' outside and reinstate him in another part of the factory.

Claude came up with a plan that would see Henry spending the winters in La Canadel and summers in the south of England, the latter house eventually being sited in West Wittering. Claude arranged that Henry would be accompanied by three designers; two draughtsmen; a housekeeper and a chauffeur; and there was a three-car garage. It seems likely that Henry would have had a hand in the design of the La Canadel house and separate accommodation for his team. He displayed another of his talents with an excellent water-colour painting of the house.

Having done his best to preserve Henry's health Claude turned his attention to the rest of the company management, instituting annual health checks and golf on Saturday, which was not to be relayed to 'Pa' Royce, who would certainly have frowned on such frivolity. He was not content with this, so he arranged for all the works staff to go to the Derby theatre once a week at the company's expense.

Claude had just settled back into his company responsibilities when he was informed that Henry had been taken ill again. On arrival at La Canadel he realized that Henry would have to return to London for diagnosis and treatment. One of the Silver Ghosts was modified to provide ambulance-style accommodation. Driving across France through the night, Henry became concerned that another car was catching up. He asked the driver to speed up but still the other car gained on them, eventually overtaking, and as it swept past Henry said 'It's all right – it's one of ours.' On arrival in London the doctors found that it was essential for Henry to have a colostomy; and it is believed that this was the first time that this procedure had been carried out in the UK.

On his recovery Claude appointed a full-time nurse, Ethel Aubin, who would remain with Henry for the rest of his life. She did not have an easy task, particularly in trying to keep him to sensible hours. One example of this occurred at West Wittering. Henry had been out for an evening walk, probably reviewing his wheat field, which was admired by local farmers. Nurse Aubin became concerned when it got dark and went out to find him. She heard noises emanating from his workshop, and there she found him in the process of making new hinges for the garden gate that had not closed properly. Henry explained 'It was a poor design that had to be corrected.'

With the outbreak of war in 1914 car production ceased, although a number of Silver Ghosts gave sterling service at the front throughout the war as staff cars. Claude managed to get contracts for shell casing manufacturing and for converting Silver Ghost chassis to armoured cars. These latter were very successful, particularly with Lawrence of Arabia's forces. A few of the same cars were still in use in the Middle East at the start of the Second World War.

The Ministry then asked Henry Royce to produce the French Renault 200hp aero engine under licence. Henry, who previously had refused a plea by Rolls to produce aero engines, now stated he would produce a better engine. This was a 20.3-litre V12 designed for a 200hp output. Six months later Ernest Hives was able to report that on its first run it had developed 250hp, and it would eventually be developed to achieve 360hp. This engine powered the twin-engine Vickers Vimy, which made the first transatlantic flight in 1919. The Vimy went on to pioneer routes to South Africa and Australia. Claude decreed that all Rolls-Royce aero engines would be named after birds of prey. This engine, the Eagle, was followed by the 14.7-litre Falcon. This engine in the Bristol fighter produced the best fighter aircraft in the later stages of the First World War. The Hawk, based on one six-cylinder block from the Falcon, was used through-out the war on Royal Navy 'Blimps' (non-rigid dirigibles). Post-war engines were the Condor and the very successful Kestrel. So by the mid-1920s Rolls-Royce was an established aero engine and car manufacturer.

In 1927 the Supermarine S.5 seaplane, designed by R.J. Mitchell, had won the International Schneider Trophy race. For the 1929 race Mitchell needed more power than the Napier Lion engine could produce. Royce, facing great opposition from the Board who were convinced that the future of the company lay in the cars, went ahead with the design of the Buzzard, a 37-litre V12 scaled up from the Kestrel. This would form the basis of the 'R' racing engine. Although some preliminary work on the 'R' was undertaken, this ceased when Vickers, the new owners of Supermarine, refused to fund any further work.

At this stage it is necessary to look at the most significant changes that would ensure that Rolls-Royce continued as a major producer of aero engines. Firstly the Chairman of the company had resigned and was replaced by A.F. Sidgreaves who was conscious of the need to restore the ailing Aero Engine Division. Secondly, largely instigated by Hives, a number of eminent engineers had been recruited, mainly to work on aero engines. They included A.G. Elliot, Cyril Lovesey, A.A. Rubbra, Ray Dorey, and Colonel L.F.R. Fell. The latter had been Assistant Technical Director at the Air Ministry and his first action was to set up an Aero Engine Sales Department. His links with the Ministry and RAF were to prove very important. One of his ambitions was for the British team to achieve two more consecutive victories in the Schneider Trophy races to give them the trophy in perpetuity.

In 1928 the reconstituted board had decided to go ahead with the Buzzard and, driven by Hives, the engine was on test in the remarkably short time of three months from initiation of the program; it developed 825hp. In November of that year the Air Ministry decided to back the RAF High Speed Flight team for the 1929 race.

Major Bulman, Deputy Director R&D (engines) in the Air Ministry, who would later become a significant contact for Rolls-Royce, asked Henry if he could build the 'R' engine in time. He said 'He could and he would'. As we have seen, due to his ill health Henry had spent several years living in the south of France in the winter and at West Wittering in the south of England in the summer. It was at this latter residence that he gathered his team of engineers for detailed discussions on the 'R' engine programme. He took them to the beach where he used his cane to sketch the S.6 nose in the sand. From this he deduced that due to the longer reduction gear of the 'R', the front of the engine would fit into the space available in the streamlined nose of the S.6 but the valve covers on each block of cylinders would need to be tapered so that they would not protrude from the cowling. He left his team to complete the design, although he still approved each drawing. The major contribution to the increase in power of the 'R' over the Buzzard was the use of a large double-sided centrifugal impeller in the supercharger, designed by Ellor and later this design was used by Frank Whittle for his first jet engines. F.R. Banks of the Ethyl Company came up with a special fuel consisting of 89 per cent benzole and 11 per cent aviation petrol plus 5cc of tetra-ethyl lead per gallon, starting an association with Rolls-Royce that would prove vital in 1940.

The 1929 Schneider race would take place at Calshot on 7 September 1929. The 'R' engine developed 1,900hp and the two S.6 aircraft had completed the preliminary flight tests on 6 September. A mechanic was changing the spark plugs when he noticed some metal fragments in one cylinder. The Rolls-Royce representative Cyril Lovesey was called to inspect the evidence and realized that the piston was damaged. The race rules did not allow engine replacement but repairs were allowed with the engine in situ. Discussing the problem with Mitchell, Lovesey said that although it should be possible to remove the cylinder block containing the damaged piston there were no mechanics on site that were competent in this work. This impasse was resolved when they were told that a party of Rolls-Royce mechanics had come down from Derby to witness the race. Lovesey found three of the party who had not been drinking, one of whom was Jack Warwick who went on to become manager of the Experimental Department. Another stroke of luck was that one of the three was left handed and could remove the gudgeon pin, releasing the damaged piston. When the work was finished Lovesey ran up the engine and declared all was well. The S.6 went on to win the race and later set a new world speed record of 357mph. As a result of this triumph Henry Royce received a knighthood.

Any thought of an outright win at the 1931 Schneider Trophy seemed to be dashed when the newly elected Labour Government refused any funding. However, the intensely patriotic Lady Houston learned of the situation and put up £100,000 saying 'Every last Briton would rather sell his last shirt than to admit that England could not defend herself before all comers.' This seemed rather an over the top statement, although it should be remembered that the rival Italian team had the full backing of Mussolini. Once again, it was a race against time for Mitchell to design the new S.6b seaplane and for the 'R' to be up-rated. Henry's team strengthened every stressed part in the engine; the supercharger was run at a higher speed and F.R. Banks produced an even more exotic fuel. Armed with no less than 2,350hp, the 'R' engine was ready just a few days before the race. In the event the race was a walkover as the Italians withdrew their entry.

The S.6b, following the race victory, set a new world speed record of 407.5mph with a sprint version of the 'R' developing 2,800hp. The 'R' engine went on to eventually become the only power plant to be used in the machines that held the world record in the air, on land and water.

The Land Speed record was a competition between two British cars using the 'R' engine. Sir Malcolm Campbell made several successful attempts with his Campbell Napier Bluebird car powered by one 2,350hp 'R' engine, culminating in 1938 with a record 301.337mph

Captain George Eyston was probably the most prolific car speed record holder in a huge variety of classes starting in 1921. His 1938 eight-wheel car, Thunderbolt, powered by two 2,350hp 'R' engines, took the record from Campbell, who had loaned him one of his 'R' engines as a spare, with a speed of 357.50mph.

In the Water Speed record there were three competitors using 'R' engines. Miss England II, powered by two 'R' engines rated at 1,800hp and driving a single propeller, set a new record at 98.76mph on 13 Friday June 1930 piloted by Sir Henry Segrave.

Following the record run he attempted another and was killed, together with Rolls-Royce engineer Vic Halliwell, when the boat capsized, probably due to striking debris. Miss England II was rebuilt as Miss England III and with the 'R' engines rated at 2,000hp, driving twin propellers, set a new record of 119.81mph piloted by Kay Don. Sir Malcolm Campbell, in his Bluebird K4 boat, powered by one 2,350hp 'R' engine, set a new record of 141.74mph in August 1939. The secret of his success was the use of a three-pointer hydroplane hull design. A total of twenty 'R' engines were produced and all this high-power experience contributed to future Rolls-Royce aero engine design, not least in the areas of materials and supercharging.

We need to go back to 1925 to appreciate that there was recognition amongst some that a more powerful engine would be needed for the RAF's 1930s combat aircraft. Air Marshal Trenchard and the Air Ministry had raised this issue with Rolls-Royce, but no follow-up action was taken. It was left to Sir Henry Royce and Ernest Hives, who believed that the excellent Kestrel was too small for further development, to go ahead with a new larger engine. Late in 1932, lacking any sign of interest from the customer, Hives had a meeting with the sick and ageing Royce, which resulted in the decision that the company should go ahead on its own initiative with the P.V.12 (Private Venture 12 cylinder), a supercharged 27-litre V12 targeted for the 750 to 1,000hp range. Design was split between the small team based with Henry in West Wittering and the Derby team. It was a typical Royce design, the two banks of six cylinders having two inlet and two exhaust valves per cylinder operated by single overhead camshafts, a centrifugal supercharger, and an SU carburettor. The Merlin was originally designed with steam cooling, a system that removed the need for drag-inducing radiators. Flight testing of this system was carried out on the Goshawk engine (a development of the Kestrel) in a number of prototype aircraft up until 1934. It was finally abandoned due to the inability to cope with the lower aircraft speeds in climb and the weight penalty. The Merlin was eventually changed to glycol coolant during its development testing.

Henry Royce died at West Wittering on 22 April 1933, the day the last P.V.12 drawing was completed. As we have seen, he left behind a strong team of managers, designers and engineers. His design team now moved to Derby and A.G. Elliot became Chief Engineer.

Two P.V.12 engines were built and the first engine run took place on 15 October 1933. At this point the company accepted the offer from the Air Ministry to finance development; as a result the P.V.12 was named the Merlin (after the bird of prey not the magician). In July 1934 the first type test was completed at 790hp. An engine was installed in a Hawker Hart light bomber for a first flight on 21 February 1935. The Rolls-Royce test pilot reported the remarkable rate of climb in this biplane.

A gifted designer, Elliot was recruited from Napier in 1912 and immediately appointed to Henry's team where he was initially involved with the Silver Ghost developments. In his Chief Engineer role he concentrated on the Merlin project. He went on to become a Director; Joint Managing Director with Hives, and finally Executive Vice Chairman to Hives until his retirement in 1954. Some other members of the 1933 team are worthy of mention due to their significant input to the Merlin.

R.W.H. Harvey-Bailey joined Rolls-Royce in 1910 as Chief Technical Production Engineer. His main task was translating Henry's designs to production; he was also a specialist in materials. He was given responsibility for scaling down the Eagle to the Falcon and later was involved with the Condor, Buzzard, Kestrel and 'R' engines. Throughout this time he was also working on the car projects. In 1933 he became involved with the Merlin mainly on production procedures and materials. He was made Chief Engineer of the car Chassis Division in 1937. With the outbreak of war he was moved back to aero engine work, which saw him in charge of material and quality control, repair engineering and service engine defect investigation. He retired aged sixty-nine in 1945.

Cyril Lovesey was a Bristol University BSc graduate who joined Hives in the experimental department in 1923. He was an ingenious engineer, particularly in engine development; an example of this was on the Kestrel engine when changes to the rather inaccessible twin carburettors were being evaluated. He ran the engine with one block of cylinders and its associated pistons and con rods removed with the respective carburettor blanked off; this allowed changes to be made rapidly. Another example is the piston replacement on the 1929 Supermarine S.6, which is described earlier. In 1931 he joined the Flight Test Department at Hucknall. During this time he learned to fly and purchased a de Havilland Gypsy Moth, which he flew until 1939. His stay at Hucknall was short and he returned to Derby to work on the Merlin, which was giving problems with the evaporative (steam) cooling. He knew how the Americans were tackling the cooling problem and suggested the use of ethylene glycol, which allowed higher temperatures and smaller, lower drag airframe radiators. This evolved as pressurized water cooling with 30 per cent glycol as an anti-freeze. In 1940 he took charge of Merlin development through all the power increases, and at the end of the war he undertook development of the Merlin for civil aircraft use. He then played a major role in the jet engine, becoming Chief Designer Projects in 1947. In 1957 he became Chief Engineer (aircraft engines); Deputy Director of Engineering and joined the Aero Division Board.

He retired in 1964 but was retained as a consultant. I had the privilege of meeting Cyril Lovesey on two occasions. The first, in 1950, was somewhat embarrassing. As an engineering apprentice I was working in the compressor office, plotting compressor outlet pressure contours, when a fairly small man in a brown suit with a rather battered trilby asked if I knew where Geoff Wilde (the department head) was. Taking him for a millwright I said, 'Sorry, I don't.' He asked, 'Well, could you find him?' Full of the importance of my job, I replied 'No, I am too busy. If you wait outside his office he will be back soon.' Shortly afterwards he came back accompanied by Geoff Wilde, who introduced him and told me he was Lovesey Chief Designer Projects. Abject apologies from me were greeted by 'Not at all; I appreciate your dedication to your work', accompanied by a handshake and charming smile. In 1965 I arranged to meet him at his home for advice on a problem on the Dart Turboprop water-methanol injection system. He remembered me and said, 'I was right. I told Geoff that you would do well in the company.' Having suggested a simple solution to the problem he then entertained me for an hour or so – a truly remarkable man.

Ray Dorey was another Bristol University graduate who was taken on by Hives in 1927 to work in the Experimental Department. He made rapid progress and by 1929 was in charge of the intensive testing of the 'R' engine for the Schneider Trophy race. In 1931 he was appointed Installation Engineer and tasked with advising aircraft manufacturers on the advantages of liquid-cooled engines with their small frontal area and hence low drag compared with air cooled radial engines. In 1935 he was appointed manager of Hucknall Flight Test, which at that time consisted of three aircraft: a Hawker Hart, Hawker Fury and Gloster Gnatsnapper. He added a Hawker Horsley that was more suitable for endurance tests due to its long range, demonstrated when 100 hours were flown with a Merlin II in six and a half days. The next addition was the low-drag Heinkel H70 fitted with a Kestrel and later a Goshawk engine. When Hives became General Manager he decided that the design of power plant installation should be carried out at Hucknall. With the outbreak of war, activity increased rapidly with prototype installations for such aircraft as the Merlin-powered version of the Beaufighter. A Hurricane repair line was set up and later the first conversion of a Spitfire Mk I to Mk V was carried out followed by the conversion of a Mk V to a Mk IX with two-stage Merlin. In October 1942 the installation of the two-stage supercharged Merlin in a North American Mustang in place of the Allison engine resulted in the P51D, the outstanding long-range fighter aircraft of the Second World War. With the onset of the jet age the test flying at Hucknall increased with a variety of test aircraft, to cover both turbojets and turboprops. Dorey's achievements during his time at Hucknall were truly amazing. He returned to Derby in charge of Nene, Tay, reheat and Dart development, Finally, in 1951 he became General Manager of the Motor Car Division at Crewe where Hives saw that his dynamism would strengthen the management team. He retired in 1968.

These are a few of the outstanding engineers who were involved in the design and development of the Merlin engine.

Back to 1935, the next variant of the Merlin was tested in February 1935 and delivered 950hp. Several design changes were made and the Merlin C was tested in April 1935. By this time the Merlin had been selected for the Hawker Hurricane, the Fairey Battle and the Vickers Supermarine Spitfire, in the latter case a private venture between Vickers and Rolls-Royce. The Hurricane first flew on 6 November 1935 and the Spitfire on 5 March 1936. Early flight tests revealed mechanical problems in the Merlin, which reached crisis proportions when the Hurricane and the Fairey Battle light bomber production lines were being held up. Fortunately, in 1937 Ernest Hives was appointed General Manager of Rolls-Royce, and he immediately separated the car and aero engine work. He instructed a scaled-up Kestrel one-piece cylinder block to replace the troublesome separate head on the Merlin, together with other modifications. The Merlin Mk I passed its 150-hour type test in November 1936. This was followed in quick succession by various improvements resulting in the Merlin Mk II with a maximum power of 1,030hp and the first engine with a two-speed supercharger, the Mk X with a maximum power of 1,145hp, the latter destined for bomber applications.

By the outbreak of war a total of 4,800 engines had been delivered, mainly Mk II and Mk X standard. However a proposed 'Speed Spitfire' for an attempt on the airspeed record resulted in the development of one of the most powerful Merlins ever built. It was a strengthened Mk II running at very high boost pressure on an exotic fuel. It delivered 2,160hp and, more importantly, it was put through an endurance test at 1,800hp, demonstrating the inherent strength of the design. Most of the strengthening improvements in this engine were incorporated in production Merlins. The record attempt was abandoned due to the successful German efforts and the outbreak of war.

Recognizing the importance of the Merlin, it was clear that additional production capacity would be required over that available at the Derby factory. Shadow factories were constructed at Crewe in 1937 and Hillington, Glasgow, in 1939. Ford commenced Merlin production in Manchester and the Packard Company in the USA produced its first Merlin in 1942.

It was appreciated that the current 87 octane fuel was limiting the boost pressure and hence power, due to detonation ('knocking' or 'pinking'). A crucial breakthrough in fuel processing in the UK in 1935 led to the USA developing a 100 octane fuel. F.R. Banks of Schneider Trophy fame was urging for the RAF to be provided with 100 octane fuel. The Air Ministry obtained samples of the fuel from America, and Rolls-Royce and the Bristol Aeroplane Company carried out tests. Problems with variations in anti-knock performance were resolved and the resulting fuel was given the British Specification DEngRD 2485. With this fuel the Merlin combat boost pressure could be increased from 6psi to 12psi, giving a 30 per cent increase in power. Another change to the exhausts from plain slit type to ejector type gave a useful increase in airspeed of 15mph. These changes, together with the Rotol variable pitch propeller were vital in the Battle of Britain.

Throughout the war the Merlin was able to match or exceed the power of the Messerschmitt 109 Daimler-Benz DB 601 and DB 605 engines, which had a capacity of 36 litres compared with the 27 litres of the Merlin. With the introduction of the two-stage, two-speed supercharger and 150 octane fuel, power had reached over 2,000hp by the end of the war. Hives had recruited Dr Stanley Hooker, a brilliant mathematician, from his position as Senior Scientific Officer at the Admiralty Research Laboratory. The story of his recruitment is worth repeating. He was first approached by Dr Fredrick Llewellyn Smith, a friend from Oxford University days. This led to an interview with Colonel Barrington, at that time Chief Designer; he did not hear anything for two months. However, he was then summoned to see Hives. The interview seemed to get off to a poor start; Hives having read two of Hooker's books asked him to describe a Karman Vortex Street (fluid dynamics study of uneven spiral vortices generated by reaction with blunt surfaces). Hives was assessing Hooker's knowledge relative to supercharger efficiency. After Hooker's attempted explanation, Hives said 'You're not much of an engineer are you?' When Hooker wrote his autobiography years later, he used this phrase as the title. Having explained that he had plenty of engineers but felt that mathematicians and scientists would be needed in future, Hives offered Hooker the job. Somewhat surprised at the brevity of the interview, Hooker asked what the salary would be. Hives asked him for whom he worked, and immediately phoned Charles Wright at the Admiralty. The conversation was brief. Hives said, 'I have a chap called Hooker here who says he works for you; he wants a job with us.' Having elicited the information he required he persuaded Wright to release Hooker. A handsome salary of £1,000 was agreed and Hives then regaled his new employee with the Royce ethos, his own open management style and the task that lay ahead.

On a cold damp day in January 1938 Hooker walked up a dismal Nightingale Road towards the factory entrance; like Hives thirty years earlier, the further he walked the more he had misgivings. Surely this could not be the home of the great Rolls-Royce? He was shown into A.G. Elliot's office, who had him taken to his new small office. Here he waited for someone to tell him what he would be doing; to show him round the premises and introduce him to his new colleagues Nothing happened and he learned later that this was a deliberate policy on the part of Hives, to allow for initiative to play its part in finding the right area in which to work. The next day he wandered around and finally met a man who was involved with the Merlin supercharger. Having studied the drawings he saw that a change in the matching of the diffuser and impeller, plus moving the airflow entry point to the centre of the impeller, would result in a significant improvement in efficiency. He checked his calculations and was delighted when his suggestions were swiftly approved. This was followed up later with the two-stage supercharger.

The mathematics involved in his supercharger performance calculations read across to the jet engine. Hooker, having met Frank Whittle, persuaded Hives that this would be the power plant of the future. Hooker went on to be one of the most formidable contributors to the jet engine era, with Rolls-Royce and Bristol, and was knighted in 1974.

The new two-stage supercharger was the result of the Air Ministry requesting a turbo-charged Merlin for a proposed pressurized, high-altitude, version of the Wellington bomber. Rolls-Royce was loath to go down the turbo-charged route and Hooker's two-stage super-charger met the requirement. However, the Wellington project was cancelled.

Discussing the wasted effort at his regular Monday management meeting Hives asked, 'What would happen if we put this engine in the Spitfire?' There was some consternation amongst the assembly 'Why had nobody thought of this before?' Hucknall designed the installation in a Mk V Spitfire and renamed it the Mk IX. This aircraft proved to be the much needed equal of the FW190.

One 'dog fight' problem with the Merlin was the momentary negative-g cut out when pushing over into a dive in pursuit of the enemy aircraft. This was due to a weak fuel flow to the engine resulting from negative-g causing reduced flow from the float chamber of the SU carburettor. The Me109 did not suffer this problem because the DB 601 engine used fuel injection. Miss Shilling of the Farnborough Research facility came up with a temporary solution, consisting of fitting a diaphragm with a calibrated hole in the float chamber, which reduced the under-fuelling in negative-g. My father, who was a Rolls-Royce liaison specialist, assisted Miss Shilling with the trial installation in a Spitfire. She caused a stir at the RAF station, arriving on a powerful motorbike (she raced motorcycles before the war). The modification was applied to all Fighter Command aircraft by March 1941. After the war they met up again when she was racing a Lagonda Rapier car. It is presumed that she would have been involved in the Farnborough-inspired modified SU carburettor, which overcame most of the negative-g problems. The final complete solution was the adoption of the American Bendix-Stromberg injection carburettor in 1943, and later by the SU Injection Carburettor.

Although the Merlin was only used in the Battle of Britain in the Hurricane, Spitfire and in the relatively short involvement of the Defiant, it also powered bombers, initially the Fairey Battle, A.W. Whitley and some versions of the Vickers Wellington and Handley Page Halifax, then later the majority of Avro Lancasters and all Mosquitos. One of the most important applications was initiated by Ronny Harker who was the Rolls-Royce liaison pilot who flew all new RAF aircraft. One of these was the Mustang, which had been ordered by the Air Ministry from the North American Aircraft Company. This had been relegated by the RAF to a ground attack role due to its poor altitude performance. He flew the aircraft in April 1942 and was very impressed with its low level performance and overall handling and suggested to Hives that the installation of the latest two-stage two-speed supercharger version of the Merlin would transform its performance. Hives immediately contacted the RAF for the loan of an aircraft for a trial installation of the Merlin 61 at the Hucknall Rolls-Royce facility. Three aircraft were converted relatively easily; a major change moved the carburettor air intake mounted on top of the cowling to a position below the cowling to suit the Merlin; giving a marked improvement to the line of forward sight for the pilot. After some American resistance to this project, two of the modified Mustangs were sent to the USA. And so was born the most outstanding long-range escort fighter of the Second World War, the Mustang P-51D.

A total of just under 170,000 Merlins were produced during the war, powering over thirty types of aircraft, including such icons as the Mosquito. A private development by de Havilland was the Hornet. It was based on the Mosquito wooden construction and originally designed as a single-seat long-range fighter; although some were modified to include a bubble cockpit for an observer behind the pilot. It was powered initially by Merlin 131 (left hand rotation) and 132 (right hand rotation) engines developing a maximum power of 2,070hp. The coolant pump was repositioned and the air intake changed to a down-draught configuration to provide a slimmer nacelle. The Royal Navy Sea Hornets were equipped with 133 and 134 Merlins down rated to 2,020hp.

The prototype's first flight took place in July 1944 and it achieved a speed of 485mph, a record then for twin-engine aircraft; in production form the speed was reduced to 472mph. Test pilot Eric 'Winkle' Brown praised its excellent handling and manoeuvrability during a trouble free aircraft carrier test programme. Armed with four 20mm cannon and capable of carrying two wing-mounted 1,000lb bombs or eight rocket projectiles and having a range of 3,000 miles, it was a formidable aircraft It was modified for the Royal Navy with folding outer wings and the aircraft was evaluated by the Canadian and Australian Navies.

The variants and production numbers (in brackets) were:

RAF– F1 Fighter (60); F3 fighter bomber (132); FR4 fighter/ reconnaissance (12): PR2 photo reconnaissance (5).

RN – (Sea Hornet) F fighter (73); NF21 nght fighter (72); PR photo/reconnaissance (23).
Overshadowed by the onset of jet-powered aircraft, this remarkable and elegant aircraft was withdrawn from service in mid-1956.

Two unusual post-war applications for Rolls-Royce were in the Spanish-built Heinkel 1-11 and the Me109. These aircraft were employed in the production of the *Battle of Britain* film.

An unsupercharged version of the Merlin, known as the Meteor, powered the Cromwell tank; also during the war, a marine version was developed for motor torpedo boats. There was even a proposed application for use in a large torpedo! There was general agreement, amongst experts from both sides of the warring factions, that the Rolls-Royce Merlin was the best engine in use during the Second World War. Post-war, the Merlin was fitted to civil aircraft, the Avro York and Lancastrian (both based on the Lancaster bomber), the Avro Tudor and the Douglas DC-4M. Apart from these applications the Merlin was used in the post-war years in high-speed racing boats and still flies today, in highly tuned form, in racing Mustang aircraft, not forgetting the vintage Spitfires, Hurricanes and the lone Lancaster that thrill spectators to this day.

This is a fitting tribute to the memory of Sir Frederick Henry Royce, a man who rose from humble beginnings to become recognized as a genius in piston engine design, and to his team, led so ably by Ernest Hives, from inception to its ultimate development.

Chapter 3

Sydney Camm –
The Designer of the Hurricane

The man

'From Little Acorns Mighty Oaks do grow'.

On 5 August 1893 at 10 Alma Road, Windsor, Sydney Camm was the first of twelve children born to Mary and Frederick William Camm. Sydney was educated at the Royal Free School between 1901 and 1908, and at fourteen he left with a high opinion of the school. His younger brother Fred was just as bright as Sydney and later became editor of the popular *Practical* magazines.

Their father was a skilled hard-working carpenter who showed them the need for accuracy and quality. This was the time for aviation with all its great potential, and he spent hours whittling model aeroplane propellers. The Wright brothers had designed, built and flown their successful controllable powered aeroplane on 17 December 1903 so everyone, everywhere, wanted to get flying!

Sydney's lively and lifelong interest in aviation started when he saw drawings of a Wright Flyer at a nearby model shop, published by those famous model makers, Bassett-Lowke. He made a model, but it didn't fly very well, but he persisted and made one from *Daily Mail* drawings, which came out after Louis Blériot's cross-Channel flight. His great interest was reinforced as he read two new magazines, *Aeroplane* and *Flight*. Their content and brilliance lasted for many years.

The brothers became good craftsmen in their own right and built reliable model aeroplanes for Herbert's shop in Eton High Street. Their biplane and monoplane models were advertised 'Will really fly' and 'Will rise from the ground'. But they also acquired a sense for business as a better price could be got by direct sales to the Eton boys. Many models were delivered at night, lifted up to the Eton dormitories by string to avoid the attention of the school authorities. Of course, the owner of Herbert's shop wouldn't have been too pleased either!

So, from his time at school, Sydney showed a keen interest in aviation, founding the Windsor Model Aeroplane Club, when he made successful rubber-driven model aircraft. His biplane gliders also flew during the weekly meetings held in Windsor Great Park, the foundation of his career as one of Britain's greatest aircraft designers.

Sydney's life gathered speed as he and his friends built a man-sized glider. He planned to fit an engine in it, and there is a plaque in Athlone Square, Ward Royal, reading 'In a building on this site Sydney Camm designed and built his first powered aircraft in 1911–1913.' Sadly the project, using a 20hp two-stroke engine, never even took to the air as it was short of fabric.

Blériot's cross-Channel flight in 1909 and Tom Sopwith's landing close to Windsor Castle in February 1911 opened Sydney's eyes. He went to Brooklands and Hendon flying displays, and his interest in aviation increased. Adolphe Pégoud's inverted flying and loop in a Blériot in September 1913 impressed him most of all. Sustained inverted flying requires both carburettor and fuel feed modifications, so it is hard to understand how it was possible then.

Major pioneers in aviation, Thomas Octave Murdoch (shortened to Tommy) Sopwith and Frederick or Fred Sigrist, influenced Sydney firstly in rousing his interest, and later guided his career towards management. Before the First World War, he saw the Sopwith Tabloid flying. This was a neat, light racing biplane. Its performance for 1913 was far better than any other plane of its time. Converted to a seaplane, it won the Schneider Trophy at Monte Carlo early in

1914. The Tabloid was obviously going to be useful to the Royal Flying Corps and Royal Naval Air Service, and so it proved.

At the outbreak of war in 1914 the RNAS used Tabloids in the earliest bombing raids of the First World War against airship sheds at Düsseldorf and Cologne, to worry the Germans operating bases near the North Sea. The first RNAS raid on 22 September 1914 was unsuccessful, but in the second Düsseldorf raid on 8 October Lieutenant Marix destroyed a shed with the Zeppelin in it. Machine gun fire only just missed him, and left his rudder stuck straight ahead. He was heading deeper into Germany but he managed to turn the Tabloid round on wing warping alone. He force-landed in Belgium but the Germans were close behind so he had to abandon the Tabloid. He first took a bike, then a lorry, and managed to get back to Ostende in one piece. Lieutenant Reginald Leonard George Marix later rose to the RAF rank of Air Vice Marshal.

The RFC were less glamorous, experimentally using Tabloids as armed scouts. The Tabloid was one of the first aircraft with a machine gun firing through the propeller.

Early aviation with its daring inspired Camm to join Martinsydes, a Brooklands company with a factory at Woking, as a woodworker in 1914. He was quickly promoted to their drawing office as he came to the notice of G.H. Handasyde, at that time a leading aircraft designer. The firm constructed several fighters. As part of his work Camm inspected captured German aircraft shown at the Islington Agricultural Hall, and that must have given him a few ideas.

To cap his success in finding just the job he wanted, he married Hilda Rose Starnes at Wooburn Parish Church, Buckinghamshire, at Christmas 1915. It was a happy marriage and they both gave each other their fullest support. As time went on she, their daughter and granddaughter were always a topic in his general conversation, so he was a well-rounded man with cycling, photography and golf for hobbies.

At his work, Handasyde influenced him greatly and in turn Camm assisted him with design work until 1923. During this time they produced a glider for a competition at Itford Hill, Sussex, and achieved second place with a two-hour glide – Sydney must have been in his element.

How did he do so well? Without self motivation he would have been like so many others, grouchy and jealous. With it he became the prime candidate at any interview, with his bright background as a craftsman and model aircraft designer. As he settled into his job, he would be involved in the fabrication of a complex part, discuss it with his foreman, sketch it neatly and make a good job. There were even brighter days when his boss would mark him down as someone with great potential, as without apparent effort he showed his creative abilities and strengths, his skill and diligence. The next logical step was a move to design. But he was not a mathematical and theoretical whizz kid with formulae buzzing around in his head like excited bees, and that came with maturity. Later he would find that men with degrees were there to assist him in his office as director. When the time came he could call them his 'Young Gentlemen'.

In November 1923 Camm joined the Hawker drawing office as a senior draughtsman, taken on by W.G. Carter. Now he really was moving as Hawker, the successor to Sopwith, was one of the prime British aircraft companies. By 1925 he was appointed Chief Designer by Fred Sigrist, Hawker's Managing Director, as successor to W.G. Carter. He stayed with Hawker's for forty-three years until his death in 1966. Camm's remarkable series of successful aircraft designs ranged from the Cygnet biplane of 1924 to his VTOL P1127 of 1960, and included such great designs as the Hart and, of course, the Hurricane. The beautiful little Cygnet, his first 'solo' professional design, weighed only 375lb and was the Hawker entry for the Air Ministry Light Aeroplane Competition at Lympne in 1924.

In 1925, with Fred Sigrist, Camm developed the distinctively elegant Hawker metal construction, using cheaper and simpler jointed tubes, rather than the alternative welded structure. In the late 1920s and early 1930s, Camm designed the classic Hart family of metal and fabric biplanes. The Hart's success put Hawker in the front line of aircraft manufacturers and Camm used it as a basis for other require-ments. These included the Demon fighter, the Hart trainer, the Audax

Robert Watson-Watt, the inventor of radar.
(*Taylor Library*)

Henry Royce, the creator of the Merlin engine.
(*Taylor Library*)

Sydney Camm, designer of the Hurricane.
(*Taylor Library*)

R.J. Mitchell, the brain behind the Spitfire.
(*Taylor Library*)

Merlin engine-powered Hurricane and Spitfire. (*Planefocus*)

CH radar, transmitters on left, and the receiver towers on the right. (*IWM*)

Air Chief Marshal Hugh Dowding,
the RAF Fighter Command leader.

Air Chief Marshal Sir Keith Park,
RAF, 11 Group Leader.
(*Air Force Museum of New Zealand*)

St Paul's above London's flames and smoke. (*Taylor Library*)

The terrible retribution – Lubeck Bells, 1942. (*Lubeck Guide Book*)

Hurricane Mk II.

Hurricane Mk II B.

Flight of Hurricanes.

Hurricane Mk II C Tropical (North Africa).

Mosquito DK338.

A fleet of De Havilland Mosquitos poised for flight.

The young Tom Sopwith.

Sydney Camm at the Windsor Model Aeroplane Club, 1915.

Hawker Cygnet G-EBMB. (*BAE Systems*)

The rear fuselage assembly of the Hart and Hurricane. (*British Aerospace*)

The Flying Bedstead.

Hurricane II C.

Hurricane Mk IV with eight rockets could have two 40mm Cannon.

Mitchell and Royce at the 1929 Schneider Trophy.

Spitfire Mk II.

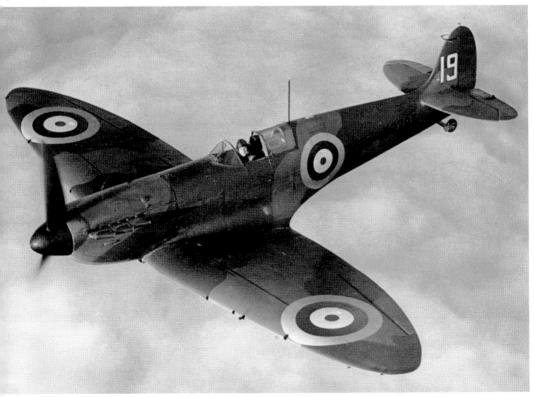

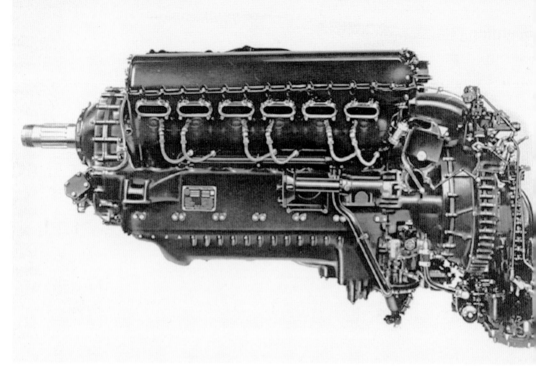

The famous Merlin engine, destined to power some of the greatest aircraft of the twentieth century.

Supermarine S.6, winner of the 1929 Schneider Trophy race reaching a speed of 328.6mph.

The iconic Rolls-Royce Silver Ghost.

The Prototype Spitfire which first flew in March 1936.

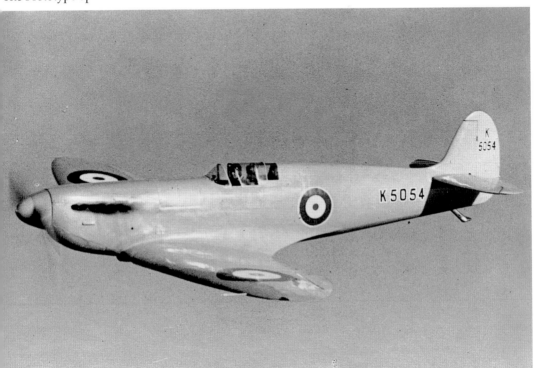

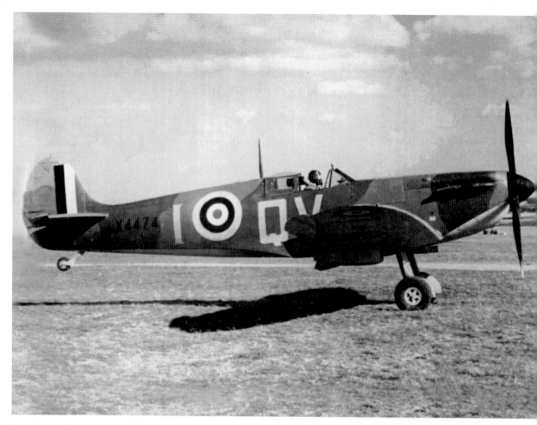

Spitfire Mk II.

The interior of a
Spitfire cockpit.
(*Taylor Library*)

V-1 Flying Bomb, also known as the 'Doodlebug'. (*Taylor Library*)

The stealthy, devastating V-2 rocket. (*Taylor Library*)

Horten 'Thousand Bomber' flying wing. (*Taylor Library*)

army co-operation aircraft, the Hind, the Fury, the Osprey and the Nimrod Fleet Air Arm machines. This new generation of aircraft boasted performance far in advance of their contemporaries. At one time in the 1930s no fewer than 84 per cent of the aircraft in the RAF were of Hawker/Camm design.

Fred Sigrist was more the driver in Hawker's technical progress, or lack of it than Sopwith. At that time Camm was not allowed the carte blanche in company policy that he later held, and he would have been given his marching orders if he tried strong arm tactics, as had proved with his predecessor, W.G. Carter. Sigrist was the director of the company and it made money, so that justified his conservative approach in aircraft design, and he reinforced the RAF prejudice against monoplanes that had persisted for many years. But with the increasing absence of Sigrist for health reasons and Camm's own elevation to the Hawker's Board, Camm eventually overcame RAF prejudice and Air Ministry apprehension, to advance from the Fury biplane. It was an excellent aircraft in its day and Camm used many of its design features in his superbly designed Hurricane. Mitchell's Spitfire and Camm's Hurricane played leading roles in the Battle of Britain, but the Hurricane shot down more enemy aircraft than all other British aircraft and ground forces combined. The two aircraft were complementary, as the Hurricane took on the German bombers, and the Spitfire went for the Bf109s, the German fighter escorts. Camm's high-performance Typhoon, Tempest and Sea Fury, were later almost as celebrated.

After the Second World War Hawker's did not rush into jet propulsion but, as always at the best time, they brought out the Sea Hawk and swept-wing Hunter jet fighters, both under Camm's direction. The Hunter, one of the longest lived jet fighters and ground attack aircraft, first flew in 1951. In 1956 I was privileged to be involved in data reduction for the Hunter partial glides at RAE Bedford, where I found its lift and drag coefficients in most flight phases. The single-seat Hunter was fitted with instrumentation, recording data on film. After a flight we recovered the data from the aircraft and *reduced* it to lift and drag coefficients for each flight. This fine aircraft could go transonic in a dive, and I vividly remember RAE

Farnborough being bombarded with its sonic boom. Controllability going through the 'sound barrier' had to be proved, so it was not just showmanship. I recall the 'Aeroplane' sketch for the SBAC show, entitled 'Here comes Bill Hunter in his Bedford!' The deliberate mix up between this beautiful aircraft and its test pilot's name, the same as a lorry shown in full bounce, was comic.

Towards the end of his career Sydney Camm was closely associated with the advanced concept of vertical take-off and landing, embodied in the P1127 aircraft. The concept was tested in the 1950s by the Rolls-Royce Thrust Measuring Rig, nicknamed the Flying Bedstead. Two Nene engines were horizontally mounted back-to-back in a steel framework on four legs. The jets exhausted downward at the centre of the rig, with one at a central nozzle and the other split, leaving through two smaller nozzles on either side. Pipes extended from the rig, using a small part of the exhaust to control the rig in roll, pitch and yaw. Gyros controlled this via pipes using servo systems. Some test flying was done at RAE Bedford from a special concrete plinth and the jet exhaust heavily abraded its edge, memorably sending dust and splinters of concrete flying.

Thrust only exceeded the aircraft weight by 600lb, and the bleed for the control pipes dangerously reduced controllability even at maximum thrust. In 1957 the test pilot, Air Commodore Larsen, supposedly failed to check the fuel, causing the accident in which he was killed. I disagree with this as I think the accident was caused by the tightening of the tether necessary for these tests. Such a snatch would only need to be a fraction of an inch to make a rate gyro give a large spurious signal, making the servo system and the aircraft topple. If you are tied to a wall by a cable and you run away, at the end of its reach the slack cable will tighten and snatch. A rate gyro is small, a handful. It senses movement, not direction. These rate gyros were fixed in the 'X' (forward/backward), 'Y' (left/right) and 'Z' (up/down) directions. If an upward movement stops sharply, then the 'Z' gyro gives a very large signal, misinterpreted by simpler, older electronics. Larsen, a wing commander when I knew him a year earlier, was a responsible person, as I demonstrate below.

The background to this tragedy had a comedic element. Larsen flew us on a Handley Page Marathon from Bedford to Farnborough in the autumn of 1956. Before departure he had mag drop trouble with one of its four engines. One of my fellow passengers, a strikingly beautiful and brilliant woman named Sheila, came out with 'What's he worrying about? He's got another three to get on with, hasn't he?' No, the Flying Bedstead accident was not caused by Wing Commander Larsen's lack of thoroughness and caution; he was far too good for that! That was why he was probably chosen as the test pilot for the Bedstead in the first place.

Camm's P1127 made its first vertical take-off in 1960. Its vectored thrust lift system replaced the Flying Bedstead's scheme, avoiding its problems. Now its jet engine exhaust gave both thrust and lift at low speeds, and the wings progressively provided a greater part of the lift as forward speed increased. The designers appreciated dangers of temporary tethers, and servo circuits limited large sensor outputs. After Camm's death in 1966 the Harrier took on the P1127's concepts, and now the P1127 prototype graces the Brooklands Museum at Weybridge. Camm's Harrier was similar to Royce's Merlin; it defeated Argentinians in the Falklands War as the Merlin had defeated Germans. Both of these brilliant machines were developed after their death.

Camm was a perfectionist rather than an innovator, but he was in advance of his time. He took care to logically evolve his designs progressively and successfully from his prior art. Although he started his career without any advanced scientific training, he had a masterful eye and an intuitive feel for a well-designed aeroplane. With such rare gifts he produced a succession of beautiful aircraft, top performers that handled well.

There is some disagreement about Sydney's character. Was he kind or was he a hard taskmaster? Once in the late 1920s there was a revolt when his well-established senior men signed a letter to Tom Sopwith asking him to moderate Camm's over-strong manner. Sydney survived, but from then on he must surely have taken a softer approach. But he never allowed any irreverence or argument from his subordinates, and before this protest he could terrify any draughtsman in a harsh dressing down. He would tear an un-satisfactory drawing from a man's board, this in the days before easy retrieval from the computer. If it was merited, the day after he would try to repair the man's self respect with an apology. He was certainly dominant, and Sopwith said years later, 'I can't imagine why his men put up with him. He was a genius but quite impossible.' In spite of Camm's later distinction, his temper did not improve, and another of his colleagues, Hawker's Chief Designer in 1965, Dr John Fozard, said of him, 'He did not suffer fools gladly, and at times most of us appeared to be fools.' But Camm's expanding team learned to respect him as leader, and enabled his company to prove the brilliance of his designs. Forceful and intolerant of any deviation, he did not want to let the smallest inferior element gain entrance to those designs.

Essentially, an aviation industry leader matures by hard knocks, almost as hard as those of any military officer, and must take on board the 'Tight Ship' approach to achieve anything at all. His academic counterpart has it easy, but aviation demands perfection. Military aviation asks for far more than this, a super perfection, that awful 110 per cent if you will, in the most advanced, reliable techniques and designs, without which aircraft are lost in large numbers to a better armed and equipped enemy. In any event, an aircraft's reputation precedes it in the counsels of the air marshals. Camm had to compete during all his time in the industry, both in his attitude and in his superb designs, and asked for perfection as he even vetted every drawing. When he had reached the top, he had to inspire his juniors to produce the best, ultimately even in the simplicity of a flat plate. Everyone in the aviation industry backs a good top designer, so on the one hand he had to jolly people along, and on the other he naturally became more abrasive and less easy-going as he progressed. The photographer shows him as a serious-minded man, but who trusts a man that smiles all the time? No doubt on occasion he could be fun, and he was broad in his interests and hobbies. But in him there was a reserve, and a steely one at that, so at the same time he came to learn from experience that he could no longer 'suffer fools gladly'. You will always find this in the managements and directorates of the aviation industry, notably in firms such as Hawker's and Rolls-Royce.

Sir Thomas Sopwith acclaimed Sydney Camm as the greatest designer of fighter aircraft the world has known. Camm received the British Gold Medal for Aeronautics in 1949 and the Paul Tissandier Diploma in 1954 from the Fédération Aéronutique Internationale. In the same year he was elected President of the Royal Aeronautical Society, and received its highest honour, the Gold Medal in 1958. Sydney Camm was knighted in 1953. He heard he was due for the Guggenheim Medal in 1965, but it was awarded after his death on 12 March 1966. Camm once said, 'The main requirements for an aircraft designer are knowledge of aerodynamics, some elementary maths, and an eye for beauty.' He could pick out a poor piece of design. His biting comments such as 'struts like floorboards' were long remembered after he had gone. He was dedicated to aircraft design for over fifty years, which led to the many honours mentioned above.

The Hurricane – the move to monoplanes

By 1933 Camm had been interested in the concept of a monoplane fighter for some time, in spite of strong Air Ministry views that the monoplane was far too dangerous as the basis for a military aircraft. This is understandable because it has no second wing to brace the first, and no support if the one and only wing is damaged. You can see that in aerial combat films – when one wing is shot away, it results in a viciously fatal, tumbling roll from which it is almost impossible to escape. However, Camm suggested a monoplane replacement for the Fury in 1933 in a meeting with Major Buchanan at the Air Ministry, and produced a basic drawing in two months, which lifted his status from pre-eminent to master at one stroke. Now he had to consider all the essential design components. You can just imagine the number of meetings he set up with his designers to decide on all the necessary requirements.

The monoplane was in, so the biplane was out! Camm would have to convince his most expert biplane designer, who would have to learn his trade again and become as expert with the monoplane. The Wright Flyer started it all as a biplane, and the Blériot mono-plane flew five years later, with the wing braced by wires above and below. Which do you choose? Evolution leads to a modern prefer-ence for monoplanes, but you can't reach up to Concorde without that essential start at Kitty Hawk. Biplane wings are simple and strong, with high drag at speed; the monoplane wings have complex internal bracing needed to give that low drag at high speed. Just compare the robust shoebox with a flat cardboard strip, or a Warren girder bridge with a Flatbed Bridge, as you visualize the cross-braced, strutted biplane, and compare it with the flimsy mono-plane. In this evolution, hybrid wing layouts take you from biplane to monoplane. The Auster was designed in 1939 as a monoplane with its high-wing braced to the lower fuselage by a strut. The Hurel-Dubois HD-32 in 1950 had slender wings of aspect ratio 32, compared with the more usual 12 or 15. These essential struts completed a triangle; the top side was two-thirds of the wing from the fuselage/wing joint to the strut/wing joint; the second side was the fuselage and the third side the strut. The outer wing, strut to tip, was not supported. The major reason for Camm's choice of monoplane was the need for low drag required by high speed military aircraft, as in the prototype that became the Hurricane. He had to jump over that middle step as he looked forward. Relatively slow biplanes such as the Fury would have been knocked from the sky! Aerial dogfights are essentially pure attrition and the fastest plane wins. Unfair? Yes, it is when you lose aircraft with the beauty of a biplane!

Manufacture and materials – simplicity or complexity

Is ultimate performance more important than easy maintenance and repair? The question is not an easy one to answer. The ultimate in performance can swing a battle in your favour, with higher speed, ceiling and manoeuvrability, but simplicity allows you to maintain and repair aircraft at a fantastic rate under battle conditions. You need metal or wood for leading edges as the use of fabric changes an aerofoil profile of the wings, tailplane and fin at high speed. But bullet holes in fabric-covered rudders, elevators, ailerons and indeed the fuselage are quickly patched; stores can be reduced too. This is obvious in the fabric-covered rear fuselage of a Mk I. Skilled fitters can run up replacements on site, instead of calling up more spares from the manufacturer. In this respect the Hurricane was the best in its day, but thankfully we had Hurricane and Spitfire squadrons to make the RAF the best.

A single-seat aircraft must be simple to fly, even if its flight systems need to be more complex to meet this need. For example, a retractable undercarriage system should only demand a simple up/down command from the pilot. He should not have to pump the undercarriage up or down, but leave the hydraulics to do that at his command. Otherwise he can't pay attention to the more important parts of his flying, such as looking out for the ground and hostile aircraft. BUMF should be no more than Brakes off, Undercarriage down, Mixture rich, and Fuel enough to go round again. Designers must incorporate this philosophy into all aircraft as much as possible.

Wood versus metal and construction details

Aircraft made of wood are light, and can be as fast as the de Havilland Mosquito, which flew at 457mph during the Second World War. Outside Europe, wood absorbs moisture and insects eat it. But light alloy corrodes as well. To avoid this, alloy components are pickled in a chromic acid bath to form a thick anti-corrosion coating. Alochrome 1200 finishes parts yellow green or iridescent blue, greatly helping paint adhesion. Alternatively, surfaces are anodized electrically in an acid bath. Light alloy naturally oxidizes to form a coat with an appreciable electrical resistance so connection can be a bit of a problem. Finally, steel can be rust-proofed, so Camm was able to combine a steel frame with wooden formers and stringers in both the Fury and Hurricane.

The Vickers Wellesley was the first aircraft to use geodetic construction. It was designed to a 1931 specification and flew in 1935, the year the Hurricane was developed. This means of construction was invented by Barnes Wallis, derived from his work on airships, of which the *R100* was the best. This design was formed from an assembly of triangles. Camm did not take it up as it originated in a competitor's patent, so that put it outside Hawker's design philosophy. Even a geodetic outer frame could not be combined with the Hawker wire-braced box frame as used in the Fury fuselage, as the two together would be too heavy. This would need larger wings so the design weight would increase. But we are jumping the gun, before we look at the load-bearing frame used in the Fury and Hurricane. This effectively combined Warren girders for the sides and rectangular girders for the top and bottom formed by horizontal cross members. These met the vertices of the Warren girder and the complete structure resembled a bridge. The whole unit was internally cross braced by stranded cables, like an elegant development of Blériot's 1909 fuselage. But the Hawker design was a major improvement, with essential work done on the prototype's attachment points, steel tubes and gussets.

Camm attached wooden formers and stringers to the box frame to create the aerodynamic shape. I should know how it went as my models were more cemented with my seven-year-old blood than balsa glue, but that means of assembly (without blood) does give a superb job. There's a fine aircraft, fabric-covered aft of the cockpit – and mine was a Hurricane in 1941 too!

Should a cockpit be open or closed? An open cockpit is simple but noisy, and the air flow can snatch a map from your hands. That must have happened to trainee pilots in Tiger Moths hundreds of times. A closed canopy is complex with a slide or hinge secured by a catch. Low drag is important for modern aircraft, so closed canopies are an obvious choice.

The Hurricane's first canopy blew off during a test flight at full throttle and rated altitude, one December Sunday in 1935. The test pilot got the aircraft back, and the redesign was perfect in RAF service. The incident appeared on the menu for the Drawing Office dinner, captioned 'Somewhere in Surrey'. In it a lady says to her husband, 'I do wish that monoplane would come again' as she tries to find space for another flower under her fine new cloche – the lost canopy.

Engine, in-line or radial

This is a significant choice because engine bearers and layouts are very different, giving two different types of aircraft, like the sleek Typhoon with its in-line engine and the 'chin' incorporating a radiator and oil cooler, or the bluff Tempest fighter bomber Mk II with a radial engine. Low drag is the major advantage for in-lines, but the Germans showed during the Second World War what they could do with the close-cowled BMW 139 radial in the FW190. Some of its features were used in the Tempest fighter bomber.

However, both radials and in-line engines powered some types. The Tempest was a case in point, as the Napier Sabre IIB engine in-line powered the Tempest Mk V and VI. Even the Hurricane itself was the subject of a design study using a Hercules radial.

The Americans preferred radials too, as in-line coolant systems were easily damaged in battle. Radial engines were more damage resistant in other ways. A British example was the Fairey Swordfish that returned with a cylinder barrel shot away during the attack on Bismark!

Camm only produced one radial-engined aircraft, his first, in 1925, before the Tempest. This was the Woodcock with a Benz engine. From then on, until after the Hurricane, all his planes were powered by Rolls-Royce in-lines. The Condor powered the Horsley, and the Kestrel powered the remainder, the Hart, the Hind, the Fury, the Nimrod and the Demon, until the Hurricane. Camm preferred Rolls-Royce from experience and he was only going to choose their brilliant new engine for his new Hurricane. This was their in-line PV12, which became the Merlin. But there was one exception: the Napier Dagger VIII 17-litre, 24-cylinder, 'H' format, air-cooled 950hp engine fitted to a Hurricane for a basic operational trainer, to ease pressure on Merlin production, but this was discontinued in November 1940.

Merlin engine types for each Hurricane mark

The Rolls-Royce Merlin was the preferred engine; the Mk I; the Merlin Mk II had the maximum power of 1,030hp at 3,000rpm and 5,500ft with 6lb boost.

The Merlin Mk III gave 1,440hp at 3,000rpm at a height of 9,000ft, using 100 octane fuel with 12lb boost for the second production batch of Hurricanes, the Mk II. These could be fitted with the Merlin Mk XX, which gave 1,480hp at 3,000rpm and 6,000ft.

The Hurricane Mk IV was fitted with a Merlin Mk 21, with a maximum power of 1,480hp at 3,000rpm and 6,000ft or the Mk 22 with a maximum 1,480hp at 3,000rpm and 12,250ft.

Note that higher boost was meant to be run only for five minutes, but could run for thirty. A long run on high boost can damage an engine, but combat is risky – it's either you or the enemy!

Fixed or variable pitch propeller

Control is important in all flight systems. An example is a properly set up automatic propeller pitch control. It does not need the pilot's attention, with fine pitch at take-off and landing speeds, and coarse pitch at higher airspeed. It changes seamlessly over the speed and height range, and the aircraft is a dream to fly. Less than that means hard work!

A solid propeller set the pitch at the start of the Hurricane development, but then it was made changeable with the de Havilland two-position propeller. With this, the pitch did not follow change in speed or height but had to be switched over, and the wrong setting could either give too long a take-off distance or a lower top speed. It was frightening for the pilot to find himself in the wrong setting, as the take-off run then ate up the airfield. Full variable pitch was introduced when new Hurricanes were equipped from their outset with Rotol constant-speed propellers on delivery to RAF squadrons from May 1940 onwards, with deliveries continuing throughout the Battle of Britain. One pilot said with heat that the Rotol propeller transformed Hurricane performance from 'disappointing' to one of 'acceptable mediocrity'. Modified aircraft were certainly popular among squadrons formerly equipped with aircraft fitted with the older de Havilland two-position propeller.

Fuselage-fitted armament

One concept never considered by Camm was the German *Schräge Musik* or 'Jazz', developed from a British First World War idea. Here the *Luftwaffe* used cannons firing upwards and forwards at 70°, which were first fitted in a radar-equipped Ju 88G-6 (capable of 400mph as opposed to the Lancaster's 275mph). With top optical gear they could aim at the wing tanks of the bomber above them, just by background light. Of course, the Lancaster bomber crew could not see the enemy at night, hiding below. This mystery weapon caused British bomber losses in sorties of between 4 per cent and 10 per cent. It's surprising that Camm did not install such a scheme in the robust Hurricane as it could have been a good platform for upward firing, easily stressed to take the guns' recoil. It would have been very effective against the Heinkel 1-11 with its wide chord wing.

The wing

Camm designed the wing simply with straight leading and trailing edges and easily draughted curves for the wingtips. He gave the leading edge a light taper and the trailing edge a medium taper. An early wind tunnel test on the wing justified a thickness/chord ratio of up to 20 per cent, later found slightly too thick. Camm chose the Clark YH (19 per cent) aerofoil, which had adequate room for armament, tyres and retraction gear. The wing looks thick in photos, but it works on all counts, being especially strong, desirable in a fighter plane. To reduce drag, the wing is finished with gussets fairing neatly into the fuselage at the trailing edge wing roots.

This aerofoil was designed in 1922 by V. Clark. The original aerofoil had a thickness of 11.7 per cent and after 30 per cent of the chord from the leading edge the lower surface was flat, allowing wing construction on a flat surface. It had a good overall performance with its high lift/drag ratio and a gentle stall characteristic. The Clark YH aerofoil was similar to the more usual aerofoils, but it had a lightly turned up trailing edge, giving it a more positive pitching moment and improved longitudinal stability. The Clark YH was already an old standard at the start of Hurricane development, but it suited it well.

The centre-section struts are part of the lower fuselage, accommodating the retracted wheels, tyres, and gear. The centre-section span was three inches less than that of Hawker's assembly hall exit, so it was a tight fit taking a partly finished aircraft out. The outer wings used a Warren girder, with front and rear main struts cross braced by diagonals, making them strong in bending and torsion, thanks to the thickness/chord ratio of 19 per cent. The angle between the diagonals and the aircraft centreline modified the pattern of the ribs they carried. The change in rib profile with span required higher mathematics to maintain the rib profile, and this was achieved by Dr P.B. Walker. The torsional stiffness of the wing had to exceed that of the aileron controls; so its fabric was replaced by light alloy stiffening the wing to retain controllability and prevent aileron reversal. The ailerons themselves remained fabric covered. A thick, well stressed wing was stronger, and it could pull more 'G' so the Hurricane, with its smaller radius of turn, was better able to turn inside its main adversary, the Bf109, a factor in its favour! The Hurricane's turning radius was 785 feet, smaller than the Spitfire's 860 feet, and much tighter than the Bf109's 895 feet. Fuel injection would have improved manoeuvrability even more in the context of negative 'g' bunts.

Camm first used a fixed undercarriage in the new monoplane as he was not convinced that better performance would follow retraction without reducing reliability. When his reservations on retraction were cleared, he advanced the monoplane design to the Hurricane concept. Two undercarriage retraction schemes were used on most Second World War fighters, outwards away from the aircraft centreline or inwards towards it, and Camm chose the second as the gear then had a wider track for better landing, which was also needed for good ground handling. This reduced the chance of ground loops on badly prepared surfaces. As he visualized, it helped when Hurricanes flew later from rough 'airfields' needed for close support in a fast moving war.

This inward main wheel retraction also reduces the aircraft's rolling moment of inertia in the air. As wheels and tyres are appreciably heavy, this improves manoeuvrability by speeding up rolls. Camm made a better choice than Mitchell and Messerschmitt in the outward retraction used in the Spitfire and the Bf109. The Hurricane's retraction gear looks light-weight and delicate, but is in fact adequately and robustly stressed. In the Mk I the main wheel tyres after inward retraction are three inches apart, and the wheel wells have a gap at the fuselage centreline. The gear takes less space in the wing, as it retracts into the fuselage more than the wing root. The disadvantage of inward retraction is the larger bending moment applied at the joint between the fuselage and wing on landing, but good stress design work takes care of that.

The new Rolls-Royce PV-12 engine overheated on the ground and at low airspeed in the airfield circuit, as it had a fuselage-mounted ventral radiator. Split flaps, duralumin skinned underneath, diverted the airflow from the radiator during slow manoeuvring, so the designers corrected this by removing the centre part of the flap to restore the radiator airflow and cure the cooling problem.

The wing's armament capacity

The whole point of a fighter is its ability to fight to its best in the hands of a good pilot. It's not meant to be a pretty demonstrator, so it must have reserves of strength and performance to take on whatever the RAF chooses for it. Incremental development on a hand to mouth basis, only just matching each requirement in turn, can be very costly and time wasting; or the aircraft type will have a very short life with a limited production run. Camm avoided this trap and managed the Hurricane design concept brilliantly with great flexibility. It was a most amazing machine, as in turn it was armed with machine guns, cannon, bombs and rockets.

The first production Hurricane, the Mk I, was armed with eight .303-inch Browning machine guns, four times the firepower of the German Bf109 with only two 7.92mm (.311-inch) MG17 guns.

In response to the Hurricane's excellent firepower, the Germans augmented these quickly by a third. The Hurricane still proved its potential as an excellent platform for most armament types.

A useful variant was the Mk IIB Hurribomber, with twelve .303 Browning machine guns in the wings. Two bomb racks were fitted outboard of the landing gear. These racks first carried one 250lb bomb each, and the bomb's weight was doubled to 500lb by the end of 1941. The Mk IIB was used to bomb small targets in occupied Europe. The next mark of Hurricane, the Mk IIC, was fitted with four Hispano-Suiza type HS 404 20mm cannon, which originated in France and fired at a muzzle velocity of 2,880 feet per second. The appearance of the IIC was obvious because the guns protruded well in front of the wing leading edges. The guns' overall length was 8 feet 2½ inches, and the recoil springs stood out. The guns were sheathed with rubber covers, and ground crews knew if a returning pilot had fired them. Its ammunition was more lethal than the Browning's, and alternated in the belt between high explosive and 20mm ball. The cannon were each armed with ninety-one rounds, making a total of 364 for the aircraft. The firing rate of 600 rounds per minute gave about thirty seconds of firing and the pilot had to be sparing with his fire. A typical burst lasted about three seconds, and a short burst one second.

The Mk IIE was fitted with a universal wing that could take 40mm guns, drop tanks, bombs or rockets, as required. It was more flexible than earlier versions, but the type was short lived, as the prototype flew on 23 March 1943, and only 270 were produced between April and summer.

The final version of the Hurricane was the ground attack Mk IV, normally armed with either 40mm cannon or rockets, on the same wing as the Mk IIE. This meant it could also take bombs or extra fuel tanks as required. It was fitted either with the Merlin 24 or 27, rated at 1,620hp. This gave the Mk IV a top speed of 284mph at 13,500 feet when carrying eight 60lb rockets and 350lb of armour. The 524 Mk IVs mostly served in the Mediterranean and Far East, as only they carried the 40mm anti-tank gun.

The tail assembly

There were no major problems with the tailplane, which was a smaller version of the wing, most notably including the Warren girder structure to which the ribs were fitted. The elevator area was about half that of the tailplane, and both were fabric covered except for the tailplane leading edge. Its elevator was free from flutter, unlike that of the prototype Typhoon. Its test pilot, Philip Lucas, only just managed to get the Typhoon back to Langley after heavy tailplane and rear fuselage flutter had severely damaged its fuselage aft of the cockpit. For his bravery he received the George Medal in 1941, a close call after his previous fright in the Hurricane due to altimeter position error.

To get back to the Hurricane, struts originally braced the tailplane to the fuselage, but were removed as they were not necessary, making the tailplane a cantilevered design. Before spinning trials the tail-wheel had been retractable, but the trials required the rear of the fuselage to be deepened by a three-inch deep ventral fin extending to the rudder. This masked the tail-wheel sufficiently so it was left permanently down.

Fin and rudder

The fin was a simple dorsal extension to the fuselage, and fabric covered except for its leading edge. It carried the rudder, comprising a vertical hinge post and second parallel member, halfway to its trailing edge at its widest point. Nine triangular ribs ran between these two, defining both its aerodynamic profile and projected shape. The ninth at the top carried forward to take the rudder balance tab. The rudder itself was shaped by upper and lower channelling either side of the balance tab. The bottom of the rudder met the ventrally finned fuselage with a tenth larger channel running between the two vertical members.

Instrumentation

The positioning of the static port in a pitot-static system is important, and must be at a point on the outside of the aircraft sensing no change in pressure due to airspeed. It may be part of a pitot-static assembly, adjacent to the pitot head as a hole on its tube, grazed by the airflow. It must never be inside the cockpit, fuselage or wing, as these act as air reservoirs, making the altimeter lag in a steep dive. Tubes linking both ports of the pitot-static head to the altimeter and ASI (airspeed indicator) must be as short as practical. The incorrect installation of the static connection in the cockpit caused the Hurricane test pilot, Philip Lucas, to have a close call as he only just missed the ground at Kenley. This was followed later by three fatal crashes of Hurricanes in early squadron service, when two pilots dived through low cloud into the ground and the third into a flat calm sea. The reason for these crashes was traced to an altimeter position error of 1,800ft when diving at about 400mph, caused by the erroneous installation of the static port in the cockpit itself. If you go from an aircraft with an open cockpit and static connection open to the air, to one with a closed cockpit, the static port must be fitted on the outside of the aircraft, a point never to be forgotten. The simplest design feature is every bit as important as the most complex, but that problem must have been a complete mystery; the crashes could have been caused in so many ways. After this point was cleared up there were no such accidents and fatalities. Company test pilots take a new aircraft over its full range. They don't just pussyfoot about, as they find the flying limits of an aircraft and look for its adverse characteristics, so that squadron pilots don't experience them. The test pilot is an expert who finds out everything there is to know about the aircraft, but he must surely take his life in his hands on occasions.

The result of all this effort by Camm and his design team is the Hurricane that we all know. It is unique and so iconic that it looks to be the easiest thing to design – you can't end up with anything else! It looked similar from start to finish, but its weight increased by 30 per cent over its design life. Camm must have been shocked to find that the weight of his Hurricane had increased a lot from its original concept. Now in war it was no longer a slim record breaker but had become a practical fighter aircraft. It was a fighter with armour plate, armament, and a powerful engine, to enable it to cause major *Luftwaffe* losses. Quick yet right design enabled Hawker's to turn out 500 more than predicted before the Battle of Britain started in 1940.

Hurricane statistics

Length – 32ft 3in
Wingspan – 40ft
Total production, all Marks – 15,195

Date	Mk	R/R Merlin engine	hp	Fuel octane rating	Boost	Top speed (mph)	Range, miles	Max take-off wt. (lb)	Armament	Notes
December 1937	I	II/III	1,030	87		324	425	6,600	Eight .303	
			1,280	100	6lb	349	425	6,600		
1940			1,310	100	12lb		425			
September 1940	IIA	XX	1,300			342	470	8,050	Eight .303	1
April 1941	IIB	XX	1,300			340	470	8,250	Twelve .303/ Four Hispano cannon	
September 1941	IIC	XX	1,280			336	470	8,100	4 × 20mm cannon & 2 × 250/500lb bombs	2
October 1941	IIB/IIC					314			'Hurribomber' with 2 × 250lb bombs	
June 1942	IID	XX	1,280			322	430	7,850	2 × 40mm cannon & 2 × .303 MG	Tank buster
March 1943	IV	24/27	1,280			330	440	8,450	2 × .303 MG. & 2 × 40mm cannon or 2 × 250/500lb bombs/ 8 × 60lb rockets/ 2 × 44/90 droptanks	Tank buster

Notes:
1. Manually switched two-speed supercharger, coolant 30 per cent glycol.
2. Alternative arrangement – eight 60lb rockets.

Hurricane development

Hurricane Mk I (early production)

The first Mk I production machines were ready fairly quickly, with deliveries from December 1937. These early aircraft featured fabric-covered wings, and wooden, two-bladed, fixed-pitch propeller. The tail-wheel was retractable, but the Hurricane needed a larger rudder area to improve the control characteristics during a spin. To get this, the lower part of the rudder was extended, fairing into the rear fuselage. This covered the tail-wheel, which was now fixed down. Early Hurricanes lacked armour or self-sealing tanks. They used 'ring and bead' gun-sights, with the ring mounted above the instrument panel and the bead mounted on a post above the engine cowling. The standard GM2 reflector gun-sight arrived in mid-1939, although many Hurricanes retained the 'bead'. The fuel capacity was 97 gallons in two fuel tanks, each of 34.5 gallons in the wing centre-section, between the spars; the fuel was pumped from these into a reserve gravity-feed tank, which held an additional 28 gallons in the forward fuselage, just ahead of the cockpit. This was the main fuel feed to the engine. The 7-gallon oil tank was built into the forward, port centre-section. The early 'K' series Mk I was powered by the Rolls-Royce 1,029hp Merlin C engine; from the 'L' serial numbers the later 1,030hp Merlin II was installed. The main coolant radiator was housed in a fairing under the rear wing centre-section; the oil cooler was also incorporated in the main radiator. Handling qualities on take-off and landing were excellent due to a wide-track undercarriage with relatively wide low-pressure tyres. With this stability the Hurricane was an easier aircraft to land without ground-looping it. So during its operational life the Hurricane was able to operate from all sorts of adverse airfield surfaces with ease.

In flight the large, thick wing made the fighter a stable gun plat-form. It was armed with eight .303-inch Browning machine guns. This armament was arranged in two groups of four in large gun-bays incorporated into the outer wing panels. In 1937 this firepower was enough to out-gun the early marks of German Messerschmitt Bf109, which were equipped with only four light machine guns.

By the time of the Battle of Britain, it was obvious the Hurricane's relatively small-calibre armament could only shoot down First World War aircraft rather than the armoured, metal machines of the early 1940s. It was quite common during the Battle of Britain for German aircraft to survive numerous hits from .303-inch bullets and still return safely to base. Later Hurricanes were equipped with a more powerful arms package, initially twelve .303-inch Browning guns, and later four 20mm (.79-inch) Hispano cannon. Hurricanes built under Belgian licence by SABCA featured four 12.7mm (.50-inch) Browning guns instead of the .303-inch armament.

Hurricane Mk I (mid-late production)

In 1939 the Hurricane's engine was changed to the Merlin III driving a de Havilland or Rotol constant speed metal propeller. Ejector exhaust stacks gave extra thrust, and duralumin replaced the fabric wing covering. An armoured glass panel was incorporated in the front of the windscreen. The 'rod' aerial mast was replaced by a streamlined, tapered design. From May 1940, 70 pounds of armour plate was added in the form of head and back armour. Starting in September 1940, IFF equipment was installed. This weighed about 40lb and was identified by wire aerials strung between the tailplane tips and rear fuselage. Added weight and the aerials reduced the maximum speed by about 2mph, but the aircraft was safer for the pilots and 'friendly' on radar. Lack of such equipment had led to the Battle of Barking Creek on 6 September 1939, causing the death of Hurricane pilot, Montague Hulton-Harrop. This 'friendly fire' tragedy was almost inevitable so early in the war, with trigger-happy pilots without benefit of IFF.

About this time new VHF T/R Type 1133 radios replaced HF TR9 sets. The pilots enjoyed a clearer radio reception which was a big advantage ready for the adoption of wing formation policy through-out the RAF in 1941. The new installation deleted the wire running between the aerial mast and rudder, and the triangular 'prong' on the mast. At the start of the war the engine ran on 87 octane fuel. From March 1940, increasing quantities of 100 octane fuel, imported from America, became available. This benefited the Hurricane Is during the defensive battles over Dunkirk with an increase in supercharger 'boost' from 6lb to 12lb without damaging the engine. With the 12lb 'emergency boost', the Merlin III was able to give 1,305hp for a five-minute burst. If the pilot resorted to emergency boost, he had to report this on landing and it was noted in the engine logbook. In 1939, the RAF had taken on 500 of this design to form the backbone of fighter squadrons during the Battle of France and in the Battle of Britain. The first RAF ace of the war, a young New Zealander known as 'Cobber' Kain, flew with 73 Squadron. In June 1940, another famous ace, Douglas Bader, was promoted to Squadron Leader, commanding 242 (Canadian) Squadron flying Hurricane Is. Roald Dahl, 80 Squadron, flew in Greece and Syria, against the Germans and Vichy.

Some of the basic design elements of the aircraft dated from an earlier generation, but the Hurricane was a match to a great extent for the *Luftwaffe*'s Messerschmitt Bf109E. British ace Peter Townsend flew Hurricanes with 85 Squadron during the Battle of Britain, and demonstrated how the Hurricane's superior turning ability could offset the Bf109's higher speed. This smaller turning circle allowed a well flown Hurricane to get onto the tail of a Bf109 more quickly than a Spitfire, assuming a Bf109 pilot was unwise enough to be lured into a turning match. Depending on altitude, the Hurricane's slow acceleration and top speed, slower by 10 to 30mph, gave the Bf109 pilot the initiative when it came to breaking off or attacking during combat. At greater height the Hurricane was hard-pressed to keep up with a well flown Bf109, or even a Me110. Lower down it was a little more even. The Merlin gave more power at low altitude than the Daimler-Benz DB601 used in the Bf109, on account of a different supercharger design. The DB601A-1 only outperformed the Merlin III and XII above 15,000 feet. The Merlin also tended to cut during negative 'g' in a bunt and inverted flight, due to carburettor fuel starvation. 'Miss Shilling's orifice', a simple modification, fixed the problem. As in the chapter on Royce the problem was solved firstly by the adoption of the American Bendix-

Stromberg injection carburettor in 1943, and then by the SU injection carburettor.

Hurricane fuel tanks were vulnerable to bombers' gunfire. The gravity-feed tank in front of the cockpit was unprotected. If this was hit, fire entered the cockpit through the instrument panel and burnt the pilot. This was reported to Dowding so he made Hawker coat Hurricane fuselage tanks with 'Linatex', a fire-resistant sealant. Now they were as fireproof as the wing tanks. Before this the fuselage tank had seemed a small target, but in one month, 10 July 1940 to 11 August, bomber gunfire hit twenty-five Hurricanes and twenty-five Spitfires – downing eleven Hurricanes for two Spitfires; so seventy-five Hurricanes were fixed every month. RAF standards made pilot reports move even an Air Marshal to take action.

The biggest advantage of the Hurricane was that it was a relatively easy aircraft to fly. This was a boon when it came to squadrons being flooded with inexperienced pilots, and it was also a steady gun platform. The closely grouped, more quickly serviced .303-inch Brownings created a pattern of fire superior to that of the Spitfire, whose armament was spaced out along the wings. In spite of its vulnerabilities in the Battle of Britain, the Hurricane shot down most of the planes claimed by the RAF (1,593 out of 2,739). Hurricane fighters flew against bombers and the Spitfires attacked German fighters. By the end of the Battle of Britain in late 1940, production of the Spitfire had increased to the point where they could meet squadron needs. In June 1940, the first Hurricane Mk I 'Tropical' version appeared, with a Vokes air filter in a large 'chin' fairing under the engine cowling. Many were ferried to North Africa and Malta via France and the Mediterranean with fixed, cylindrical 40-gallon fuel tanks under each wing to extend the range. The tropical filter and fuel tanks were to be used on later Hurricane variants.

Hurricane Mk II

Although production of the Spitfire had started to increase, a Merlin XX-powered Hurricane Mk I was built and first flew on 11 June

101

1940. The improved Merlin XX had a two-speed supercharger that could have its impeller speed changed by the pilot, depending on altitude. At about 18,000 feet, it could be switched to a higher speed gearing, 'FS ratio' (Full Supercharge) for added compression. At its lower speed 'MS ratio' (Moderate Supercharge), it took less power from the engine, making it more powerful at both lower and higher altitudes, greatly increasing overall performance of the engine, peaking at 1,280hp. The bay right in front of the cockpit was lengthened by four inches to accommodate the new engine. The carburettor air intake under the forward centre-section was modified, moving back three inches. This more powerful engine was cooled by a 70 per cent to 30 per cent water glycol mix, instead of the pure glycol used in earlier Merlin versions, which had been inflammable, so the new mix was safer. The engine also ran about 70°C cooler, giving it a longer life and greater reliability.

The Merlin XX was longer than previous Marks, so the fuselage was lengthened by 4.5 inches in front of the cockpit, improving the aircraft stability with the small forward shift in centre of gravity. The increased cooling requirements required a larger radiator and a redesigned, circular oil cooler housed in a deeper, slightly wider 'bath'.

Hurricane IIA Series 1

The initial Mk II, later known as the Mk IIA Series 1, went into squadron service in September 1940 at the peak of the Battle of Britain. Hawker had long experimented with improving the armament of the fighter by fitting cannon, trying two 20mm (.79-inch) Oerlikon cannons in pods, one under each wing (one aircraft was tested during 1940 in 151 Squadron). But extra weight and drag seriously compromised aircraft performance and manoeuvrability; the limited amount of ammunition carried and the frequent stoppages of the drum-fed guns, made the arrangement unsatisfactory. A better fit was made with four 20mm (.79-inch) Hispano Mk II cannon, two in each wing, but the extra weight reduced performance. The Hispanos were designed for a rigid, engine-based mounting and so wing flexing caused problems as the weapons twisted in their mounts when they fired, causing the guns to jam because of misaligned shells. Changes made both to the Hispanos and mountings cured this problem. Small blisters on the upper wing surfaces cleared the Hispano breeches and feed motors. The first sets of Hispano wings were modified from standard Mark I eight-gun wings.

Hurricane IIA Series 2 (Hurricane IIB)

The new Merlin XX improved performance to keep the Hurricane in production. Hawker introduced the Mark IIA Series 2 with either of two wings; one mounting twelve Brownings, the other with four Hispano cannon in the original gun-bays. The first Series 2 with twelve .303-inch Brownings (four per wing in original gun-bays and two more in new gun-bays outboard of the landing lights) arrived in October 1940. The Mark IIA Series 2 also used a longer propeller spinner, later becoming the Mark IIB in April 1941. The tail-wheel recess in the ventral keel was changed and the tail-wheel leg was a levered-suspension unit with a small torque link. For North Africa the Hurricane was tropicalized as the Mark IIB, with engine dust filters and a pilot's desert survival kit.

Hurricane IIC

The Hurricane IIA Series 2s armed with four 20mm (0.79-inch) Hispanos become the Mark IIC in June 1941, using a modified wing with a strongpoint for a 500lb or 250lb bomb, and later in 1941, fixed 40-gallon fuel tanks. Its performance was inferior to the newer German fighters, so it took on the ground-attack role as the 'Hurribomber', also as a night fighter and intruder.

Hurricane IID

The Mk II was used in ground support when it was quickly learned that destroying tanks was difficult, the cannons did not have the performance needed, and bombing the tanks was almost impossible. So the aircraft now carried a 40mm cannon in a pod under each wing, cutting other armament to a Browning in each wing loaded with tracer for aiming. These Hurricanes were nicknamed 'Flying Can Openers', a play on the logo of 6 Squadron, which flew the Hurricane, starting in 1941, equipped with the Mk II from December 1942. The layout was tested on a converted Mk IIB and flew on 18 September 1941. The Mk IID version started in 1942, with additional armour for the pilot, radiator and engine. The aircraft were fitted with a Rolls-Royce gun and carried twelve rounds, but were changed to the 40mm (1.57-inch) Vickers S gun with fifteen rounds. The weight of the guns and armour protection slightly reduced aircraft performance, but it undertook anti-tank roles in small numbers during the North African campaign where, if flak and fighters were absent, it proved accurate and effective against armoured vehicles and motor transport. A wing modification was introduced in the Mk IIE, but the extensive changes made it the Mk IV.

Hurricane Mk III

The Mk III was a Mk II with a Packard Merlin engine, intended to provide supplies of the British-built engines for other designs. By the time production should have started, British-built Merlin production had increased and the idea was abandoned.

Hurricane Mk IV

The Hawker Hurricane Mk IV was the last major Hurricane design. The versions of the Mk II with modified wings for specialized use resulted in maintenance and supply problems, so it was decided to design a more standardized and universal model to be known as the Hawker Hurricane Mk IIE. After the first 250 had been built the type was re-designated the Mk IV to further reduce confusion and errors when ordering spare parts. Additional equipment included 350lb of armour plating added to the radiator housing, cockpit and fuel tanks. It was also powered by the Merlin 24 or 27 engines equipped with dust filters for desert work, delivering 1,620hp. Its new wing could be fitted with two bombs, four 40mm cannon or eight 60lb RP-3 unguided rocket projectiles as required to replace the standard eight machine guns. Many Hawker Hurricane Mk IVs were con-verted by retro-fitting the more powerful Merlin 32 engine and a four-bladed propeller into Mark Vs. In fact, most surviving Hawker Hurricane Mk Vs are converted Hawker Hurricane Mk IVs.

The Mk IV was used in ground-attack missions in the European theatre until the early days of 1944, when it was replaced by the Hawker Typhoon. French ace Pierre Clostermann recalled that the RP-3 rocket's drag limited the Hurricane's top speed to 205mph. Casualty rates for Hurricanes carrying the RP-3 were therefore extremely high due to the lethal German flak. Clostermann described a rocket attack by Hurricanes from 184 Squadron against a V-1 site on the French coast on 20 December 1943, when three of four aircraft were downed before they could attack. So with that tragic report we have nearly reached the end of the Hurricane's service history, at least in Europe, but we must never forget that the Hurricane was there when we had needed it, and let it rip the terrifyingly threatening He 1-11s out of our skies in the Battle of Britain! Its young cousin, the Tempest, took over in the later part of the Second World War, when it would race unscathed through the fiercest German ground fire. The Hurricane still played a prominent role in the Middle East and Far East. Its use had also been critical in the outcome of the defence of Malta during 1941 and early 1942.

Canadian variants

The Canada Car and Foundry Co. Ltd made the Mk X, XI and XII. The Mk X fighters and fighter-bombers, used a 1,300hp Packard Merlin 28, Bendix injection carburettor and Hamilton Standard 'Hydromatic' constant-speed propellers. Often these aircraft lacked spinners. Eight 0.303-inch machine guns were fitted in the wings. In all, 490 were built, and 150 Mk XI aircraft followed. The Mk XII was a fighter and fighter-bomber, powered by a 1,300hp Packard Merlin 29. This was first armed with twelve 0.303-inch machine guns, but later changed to four 20mm cannons. The Mk XIIA fighter and fighter-bomber used a Packard Merlin 29, and eight 0.303-inch guns.

Sea Hurricanes

Sea Hurricane Mk IA
The Sea Hurricane Mk IA was a Hurricane Mk I modified by General Aircraft Limited, carried by CAM ships (catapult armed merchantman). These ships catapult launched an aircraft, without means to recover them. If the aircraft weren't in range of land, the pilots had to bale out to be picked up by the ship. These 'Hurricat' pilots were the bravest of the brave!

Most modified aircraft had served with front-line squadrons, and one clapped-out example broke up in trials in a catapult launch. Fifty aircraft were converted from the Hurricane Mk I. The lighter de Havilland propellers were preferred to the Rotol, as it was found during tests that the weight of the Rotol unit could lead to the nose dipping during arrested landings, causing the propeller blades to 'peck' the carrier deck. The lighter de Havilland units avoided this problem.

Sea Hurricane Mk IB
The Sea Hurricane Mk IB was a Mk IIA Series 2 version equipped with catapult spools and an arrester hook. From October 1941, it was used on merchant aircraft carriers (MAC); these large cargo ships with a flight deck enabled aircraft to be launched and recovered. In total, 340 aircraft were converted for this role.

Sea Hurricane Mk IC
The Hurricane Mk IIB and IIC aircraft had catapult spools, an arrester hook and four-cannon wings.

Sea Hurricane Mk IIC
The Hurricane Mk IIC had naval radio gear. Some 400 aircraft were converted for fleet carriers.

Sea Hurricane Mk XIIA
The Canadian Hurricane Mk XIIAs were converted to Sea Hurricanes using F.37/35 cannons.

Other design variants

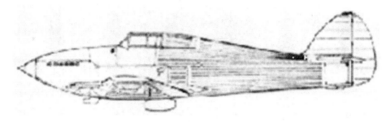

Four-cannon F.37/35
The F.37/35 four-cannon design was tested on the V7360 trials aircraft, shown on 3 March 1936. It was based on a prototype with four Oerlikon 20mm guns; it was rejected in favour of the Westland Whirlwind.

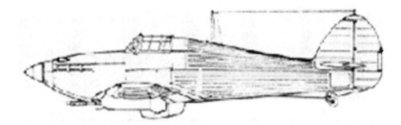

Two-cannon L1750 trials aircraft
The two-cannon design L1750 trials aircraft as it looked in 1940. It had two under-wing Oerlikon 20mm guns for its Service trials in 1939.

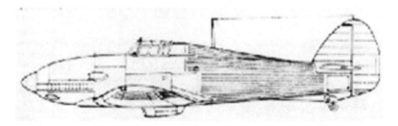

Yugoslav Daimler-Benz Hurricane
The Yugoslav DB601A in licence-built airframe before the German invasion in April 1941.

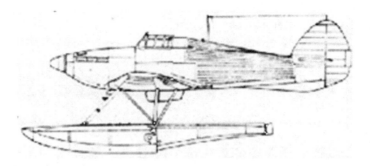

Hurricane Floatplane
The airframe was partly modified with Blackburn Roc floats delivered to Kingston. It was conceived during the Norwegian campaign but abandoned in June 1940. The designed maximum speed was 210mph at 10,000ft.

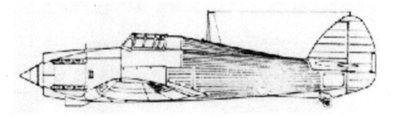

Dagger Hurricane
This was a simplified operational trainer project equipped with a Napier Dagger engine, studied during the Battle of Britain as a means of easing the pressures on Merlin production. It was discontinued in November 1940.

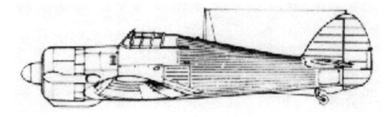

Hecules Hurricane
The Hercules Hurricane was a 1941 scheme to avoid Merlin shortages.

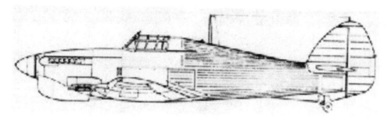

Griffon Hurricane

The Griffon Hurricane was one scheme for a four cannon development with Rolls-Royce Griffon IIA, 1939–41. It was discontinued when the Typhoon entered production.

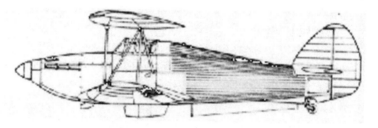

Hillson FH.40 Slip-Wing Hurricane

This was a Hawker-built Canadian aircraft modified in the UK with a jettisonable auxiliary wing to assist short take-offs and also act as an extra fuel supply. Trials were stopped in January 1944.

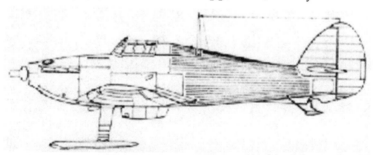

Canadian Hurricane ski landing gear

Several twelve-gun Canadian Hurricane Mk XIs were modified with fixed ski main landing gear and snow shoe tail skids. The wheel gear was deleted and wheel wells were faired over. They were equipped with Packard-built Merlin engines and Hamilton Standard propellers. They served with the RCAF in 1941–43.

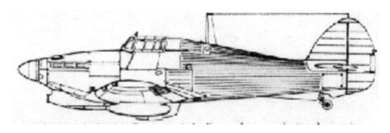

Hurricane Mk V

The Hurricane Mk V was designed for Far Eastern ground attack. Fitted with a universal wing, it was powered by a ground-boosted Merlin and a four-bladed propeller to carry heavy armour. Three prototypes were made in 1941. The Typhoon took over ground attack duties so production ended.

Hurricane Improved Canopy (Blister) Project

No picture is given for the Hurricane Improved Canopy (Blister) Project. Its reduced rear fuselage secondary structure was intended to increase field of view for intruder operations. The prototype was discontinued in March 1942. The P3899 first flew on 26 October 1940.

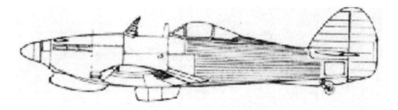

Persian Hurricane two-seat trainer

Two examples were delivered. Design started in 1939, and was completed in 1945. It was first flown with both cockpits open but was delivered with a Tempest hood over the rear cockpit. P3270 was flown by Richard Reynell at Brooklands as 2-32 on 16 May 1940; the other aircraft was 2-31.

Summary

You can see from all the variants described above that Camm and his designers, and some foreign ones too, went on from the mainstream of Hurricane production to do their best to conclusively beat both the environment and the opposition.

We must always remember our ever-reliable Hurricane; this superb aircraft had the imprint of Sydney Camm, and fought in Britain, France, Norway, Russia, North Africa, the Middle East, Italy and the Far East. It was there in France, both up to Dunkirk and later as a menacing intruder either side of D-Day.

It fought in extremes of heat and cold, wet and dry, mould and scouring sand (which can get everywhere as its particle size can be finer than quality face powder), and it proved to be among the finest, a great design. And of course, last of all, we must never ever forget its greatest contribution to winning the Battle of Britain that made us victorious.

Brilliant aircraft are no more than empty shells, and the best engines on company test beds roar loudly to no apparent effect. But, join them together in the hands of brilliant top pilots like a marriage and you have living, vibrant machines that will defeat any enemy.

And both the Spitfires and the Hurricanes did!

Chapter 4

Reginald Joseph Mitchell and the Spitfire

Reginald Joseph Mitchell was born on 20 May 1895 in Stoke-on-Trent. He was the second of five children, three boys and two girls. His father, Henry, was, at the time of his birth, a headmaster at a school. However, he soon changed careers, taking up printing; he eventually became sole owner of a printing company. As a result the children grew up in middle class surroundings. Their mother also had a strong determination and these traits were to be apparent in Mitchell in later years

Mitchell started his education at an elementary school where he showed an aptitude for mathematics. He then moved on to Hanley High School and in 1908 learned of Colonel Cody's first flight in England. This event so enthused Mitchell that, together with his brother Eric, he began to make model aircraft. These were constructed of bamboo strips and paper and, apparently, flew well. At school he showed an aptitude for sports, in particular cricket. He was a good scholar, passing his exams with ease. As a hobby he purchased pigeons and had success in long-distance races.

In this way the characteristics of initiative, determination and a competitive approach to activities were developed and would feature in his later life, There is no doubt that his parents were very influential in his development up to this stage.

In 1911, at the age of sixteen, Mitchell started an apprenticeship with the Kerr Stuart locomotive engineering company. Whilst he was not enamoured with his time in the factory workshops, this was an essential part of any apprenticeship. A move into the drawing office followed and here he began to learn the skills that would determine his future employment. He attended evening classes at a Technical School, taking courses in engineering drawing, higher mathematics and mechanics. He also manufactured a dynamo (shades of Henry Royce) and installed an electric light system to replace the gaslight in his bedroom. In 1916 Mitchell completed his apprenticeship and, whilst looking for a suitable job, he became a part-time teacher at Fenton Technical School.

In 1917 he joined Supermarine in Southampton, his personality and skills were soon recognized and in 1918 he was made assistant to the Works Manager. That same year he hurried back to his family to tell them of his plans to marry his girlfriend Flo Drayson, head mistress of a primary school. During this short visit they were married and then returned to a rented house in Southampton. Sporting and with a strong character, Flo was able to accept that for Mitchell his work was the major interest in his life.

The Schneider Trophy races (described in Chapter 2) had been won in 1913 by France, with a Deperdussin flying boat flying at 45.7mph. In 1914 the winner was a British Sopwith Tabloid at 86.8mph. After the war the race recommenced in 1919 with the Supermarine entry being a modified wartime flying boat fitted with a 450hp Napier Lion engine and some airframe improvements. It was named Sea Lion but sank after hitting an object whilst trying to locate the marker buoy in fog. The weather conditions led to cancellation of the race.

The year 1920 turned out to be momentous for the Mitchell family. The British Government issued a specification for an amphibian, leading to Mitchell's first totally original design. He undertook all the calculations himself and approved every single drawing. He worked hard and expected the same dedication from his team. When he was in a 'thinking mode' he would not tolerate any interruption. Nevertheless, after work he was happy to socialize with his team. The amphibian was a biplane powered by a Rolls-Royce Eagle VIII engine; his first contact with that company. It came second in the selection trials. In that same year his son Gordon was born and the family purchased a larger house.

There were no British entries in the 1920 and 1921 Schneider Trophy races, which were won by Italy with Savoia and Macchi aircraft; in the latter race at a speed of 117.8mph.

In 1921 Mitchell designed an improved version of his 1920 amphibian powered by a 450hp Napier Lion engine. Named the Seagull, this aircraft was ordered in quantity by the RAF and the Australian Air Force and continued in service for twenty years. The 1922 Schneider Trophy race was most significant as an Italian win would result in their retention of the trophy in perpetuity. There was no government support for a British entry so Supermarine decided that they would go it alone. Keeping the expenditure to a minimum was essential, so the decision was taken to update the 1919 Sea Lion. The 450hp Napier Lion engine was retained and Mitchell concentrated on streamlining the fuselage and flying surfaces producing a compact, 28ft wing span biplane named Sea Lion II.

The race was held in Naples with entries from France and Italy. To the evident dismay of the Italians, the little Sea Lion II won at a speed of 145.7mph. It was a close run race, beating the Italian entry by just 2.5mph; due in no small part to the superb flying skills of the Supermarine test pilot Captain Henri Biard. This was a tremendous achievement for such a small company as Supermarine. It gave Mitchell the impetus to build up a small talented team with the aim of producing more advanced designs. His first recruit was Joe Smith, a draughtsman who had been employed at the Austin car factory. Joe would go on to be a major player in the future of Supermarine.

In 1923 Mitchell designed the Sea Eagle, a six-seat amphibian powered by a 360hp Rolls-Royce Eagle IX engine. The 1922 Schneider success led to an expansion at Supermarine and Mitchell was able to recruit Alan Clifton, who became his technical assistant, and Arthur Shirvall, a former Supermarine apprentice. Arthur turned out to have a special gift for designing flying boat hulls.

Now Mitchell turned his attention to the Schneider Trophy race to be held at Spithead in September. He still favoured the flying boat design and concentrated on further improvements to the Sea Lion II.

As well as new wings he redesigned the hull and retained the Napier Lion engine, which now developed 550hp. While there was no Italian entry, the French were present and the USA entered for the first time, causing excitement with three seaplanes, two Curtiss CR-3s and one Wright NW-2. The Sea Lion was accompanied by a Blackburn Pellet as the British entries. The number of competitors was reduced as the Blackburn and the Wright crashed, and two of the French entries retired with engine trouble. The Curtiss seaplanes took first and second places with a winning speed of 177.4mph with the Sea Lion third at 155.2mph. There is no doubt that this result was a blow to Supermarine and to Mitchell in particular, as the biplane flying boat design had clearly reached its limit and the future lay with the seaplane.

In December 1924 Mitchell, aged twenty-nine, signed a ten-year agreement with Supermarine, backdated to December 1923. This agreement confirmed his appointment as Chief Engineer and Designer with a Technical Directorship, which would come into force in December 1927. This was a major confirmation of his value to the company.

He now designed the Scarab amphibian based on the Sea Eagle. This was a military aircraft, capable of carrying a 1,000lb bomb; twelve were ordered by the Spanish. This was the start of a frenetic period of design in 1924. Mitchell made full use of his team involving them in discussions of the design and encouraging their input, usually puffing on his pipe. However, he still maintained overall control of the design at every stage.

At this time another addition to his team was draughtsman Eric Lovell-Cooper, formerly of Boulton & Paul. On arrival for his interview he was put off by the state of the Supermarine buildings (like Hives and Hooker on their first sight of the Rolls-Royce factory), but all doubts vanished as soon as he met Mitchell. Together with Joe Smith, Harold Smith, and Alan Clifton, he would spend the rest of his working life with Supermarine.

The next design was the Swan, a commercial amphibian, powered by two Rolls-Royce Eagle IX engines and featuring a novel pneumatic wheel retraction system powered by an air driven propeller. This was immediately ordered by the Air Ministry and also attracted the attention of the Prince of Wales, who made a prolonged visit to the works. There is no doubt that the Swan was a most significant design as it was the foundation for the famous Southampton flying boat.

A diversion from flying boats was Mitchell's entry for the Air Ministry sponsored Light Aircraft Trial. This was a small biplane with sesquiplane wings (lower wing smaller span than upper wing). It was powered by a Blackburn Thrush, a 1.5-litre, air-cooled, three-cylinder radial engine, developing 35hp. The engine was unreliable and led to the Sparrow being eliminated from the trials; Mitchell was very disappointed by this failure. Coincidentally, another entry in these trials was the Cygnet designed by Sydney Camm of Hawker Hurricane fame.

For the 1924 Schneider Trophy the Air Ministry ordered a flying boat from Supermarine and a seaplane from Gloster. Although Mitchell had decided that a seaplane was the only way to achieve success, he did start a flying boat design powered by a Rolls-Royce Condor (600 to 705hp) and named, perhaps significantly, the Sea Urchin; this suffered difficulties in construction and was abandoned. The Gloster entry crashed and, with no entries from Italy or France, the USA team would have had a walk-over. However, they decided to postpone the event for one year to give the other teams a chance – a most sporting gesture!

Mitchell started thinking about the design of his seaplane in December 1924. He had the opportunity to examine the Curtiss machines which, although they were biplanes, were very stream-lined, had surface radiators on the wings and metal propellers. Mitchell's S.4 design was a monoplane with a cantilever wing. It had a monococque fuselage covered in plywood except for the engine bay, which used aluminium sheet closely cowled around the three 'W' cylinder blocks of the 700hp Napier Lion engine. The one-piece wing was covered in stressed skin plywood. This design was ahead of its time, a truly remarkable technological improvement; it must have made a stunning impression when it first appeared in public. The design was approved and given financial support by the Air

Ministry in March 1925. Within five months, the S.4 was ready to fly, a remarkable achievement. The initial flight test revealed some occasional wing vibration and poor visibility from the cockpit, which was set well back in the fuselage. However, it was decided to make an attempt on the world airspeed record in September, and piloted by Captain Biard a new record was set at 226.75mph.

Later in September the British team, consisting of the S.4 and two Gloster III racing biplanes, set sail for the USA. The Schneider race was to be held in Chesapeake Bay where the aircraft were housed in temporary canvas hangars. The S.4 fin was damaged on the night before the first test, a navigation flight. On 25 October a Curtiss R3C-2 was first off followed by one of the Gloster III aircraft. Next was the S.4, watched by Mitchell who was in a rescue boat. When rounding the first marker the S.4 dived into the water. Due to the rescue boat colliding with debris, it took one hour to reach the accident and Mitchell was very relieved to see Biard had survived, although he had been knocked unconscious and still strapped in, went under. The cold water revived him and he managed to undo the harness and swim up to the surface where he inflated his life jacket; a very lucky escape! Some of the wreckage was retrieved, but the cause of the crash was not positively established. Possible causes were thought to be either wing flutter or the effect of the large area of the ailerons, a necessity for take-off due to the relatively small thin wings. In later years the latter possibility found favour. The race was won by the Curtiss.

Mitchell was very disappointed with this failure but remained convinced that the cantilever wing was viable and the only way forward for high speed aircraft. However, with his next design he was back to biplane flying boats. The next was the Southampton, a development of the Swan, as mentioned earlier. This was to become the most successful flying boat built between the wars. A total of eighty-three were sold to operators in Australia, Japan, Argentina, Turkey, and the RAF who ordered six straight from the drawing board. The Southampton Mk 1 was of all wood construction, the hull being double-skinned mahogany. The Mk 2 had a duralumin hull, and the weight reduction from this change gave a 200-mile improvement in range. The Mk 3 had metal-covered wings. The majority of the aircraft were powered by two Napier Lion engines but Hispano Suiza 12NBr engines were specified for the Turkish order for six planes, and Lorraine-Dietrich 12Es for the Argentinian order for eight planes. In addition, there were trial installations of the Bristol Jupiter IX and the Rolls-Royce Kestrel. The Mk 2 had a maximum speed of 95mph, a range of 895 miles and carried a crew of five, in three open cockpits. It was armed with three 0.303 Lewis machine guns and could carry 1,100lb of bombs in under-wing installations. In 1927/28 four RAF Southamptons made a long-distance formation flight to Singapore and round Australia covering a total of 27,000 miles. The Southampton remained in front-line service until 1936.

Mitchell did not have sufficient time to design a new machine for the 1926 Schneider race and so there was no British entry. Mussolini was now in power in Italy and gave unlimited support to their team of three Macchi M.39s. The race was won for Italy, at a speed of 246.50mph, 15mph faster than the USA Curtiss machine. The Macchi went on to set a new world airspeed record of 258.87mph.

Mitchell now started preparing for his 1927 Schneider entry, the S.5. For the first time he was able to carry out a series of tests in the Farnborough wind tunnel and the National Physical Laboratory tank. There was concern over the cost of this project but the Air Ministry decided to set up a high-speed flight of RAF pilots and ordered three Supermarine S.5s, three Gloster IVBs and one Short-Bristow Crusader. All these were to be seaplanes. The S.5 had an even narrower fuselage than the S.4; in fact, rather like with Formula 1 cars, the pilots were measured to ensure they could get in and, more importantly, out without a struggle. The whole fuselage was now covered in duralumin sheet. The wings, tailplane and rudder were still of all wooden construction. Other changes compared with the S.4 were surface radiators on the wings; bracing wires between the wings floats and fuselage; the cockpit was moved further forward; and a geared engine was used to improve propeller efficiency. There had been consideration of using a Rolls-Royce engine to increase speed but it was decided to continue with the Napier Lion, which now developed 900hp. At that time there was no

Rolls-Royce engine of comparable power to the Napier. However, Henry Royce and Colonel Fell had agreed that a more powerful engine of at least 1,400hp could be produced but the Air Ministry refused to provide funding.

At this time Arthur Black, an expert metallurgist, had joined the team. He was very impressed by Mitchell whom he found made a practice of visiting the workshop every morning to closely inspect the progress of work on the S.5 in minute detail. This inspection would often result in design changes. Black was quick to appreciate the technical standards used by Mitchell and the fact that all of the members of his team were imbued with these standards (a marked similarity to Henry Royce and his team). Mitchell did have a quick temper but despite this he built up a close relationship with the team both in work and socially. However, there was no doubt as to who was the boss!

The RAF high-speed flight consisted of Squadron Leader Slatter, Flight Lieutenants Webster, Worsley and Kinkead, and Flying Officer Scholfield. Early in July Webster flew the S.5 for the first time at over 275mph and reported that it handled well. From then on the pilots flew familiarization flights in the S.5s and Gloster IVBs at Calshot. They found that once airborne the S.5 performed well; however, take-off was a different matter. Due to the torque reaction the port float tended to dig into the water; Mitchell's simple cure was to transfer fuel to the starboard float. The pilots also found that both floats threw up so much spray that visibility on take-off was severely restricted. Landing also exercised their skill to the limits, mainly due to the much higher approach speeds than they had been accustomed to. Mitchell got on very well with the RAF 'boys' to the extent that he did not mind being called 'Mitch' in spite of his normal requirement of' 'Mr Mitchell'.

On 25 September Mussolini and a crowd of around 200,000 Italian spectators gathered in Venice for the race confident of an Italian victory. Then it was announced that due to adverse weather the race was postponed until the following day. In the race two of the Macchis dropped out with engine trouble. Webster and Worsley finished first and second with the remaining Macchi in third place.

During the race Webster set a new world speed record of 281.66mph (this round a triangular course). Mussolini was not amused. However, six weeks later a Macchi M.52 set a new record at 297.76mph. In March Flight Lieutenant Kinkead made an attempt to regain the record in the S.5. He lost his life when, in diving towards the start line, he misjudged his height and hit the sea. Mitchell was devastated by this accident as he had always been conscious of the dangers involved in high-speed flight and strove to make his aircraft as reliable and easy to fly as possible. In that same month a Macchi M.52R set a new record at 318.57mph; Italy thus laying down a marker for the next Schneider race.

In November 1928 negotiations between Supermarine and Vickers were concluded with the latter company buying all the issued capital of Supermarine. One stipulation was that Mitchell should retain his position until 1933. The new company would be known as Supermarine Aviation Works (Vickers) Ltd. Shortly afterwards Sir Robert McLean became Chairman of Supermarine, a most significant appointment for future years. Vickers had an assistant designer by the name of Barnes Wallis and the Vickers Board felt that his geodetic approach to aircraft construction would work well with Mitchell's techniques. Barnes Wallis was therefore transferred to share Mitchell's office. Bearing in mind that Mitchell rejected any interruption when deep in thought, it was obvious that this arrangement would not work, and eventually Barnes Wallis returned to Vickers.

Mitchell's first design in 1928 was a development of the Southampton, named Nanook; the first Supermarine aircraft without the 'S' alliteration. Powered by three Armstrong Siddeley Jaguar engines, it had been ordered by the Danish Navy for use as a torpedo carrier. However, trials proved that it was not suited to this role and the sole example was renamed Solent and converted to a luxury flying boat for a member of the Guinness family.

When he commenced planning the design of the S.6 for the 1929 Schneider race Mitchell was reluctant to abandon the Napier Lion engine that had given such good service in his previous designs. However, after consulting Major Bulman of the Air Ministry he agreed to proceed with a Rolls-Royce engine (the 'R' racing engine is described in Chapter 2). Once again, the Government provided financial support and ordered designs from Supermarine and Gloster. The S.6 was slightly larger than the S.5; its wings and fuselage were covered in duralumin and both floats would now hold fuel. The wing surface radiators were alloy rather than copper and there were additional radiators on the floats. The fin was used as the oil tank and its surfaces as oil coolers; additional oil cooling was provided by radiators on the sides of the fuselage.

In January 1929, Mitchell was made a Fellow of the Royal Aeronautical Society (FRAeS), a well deserved recognition of his contribution to the aeronautical industry. In January the Air Ministry announced the new members of the RAF High Speed Flight. Led by Squadron Leader Orlebar, the pilot team consisted of Flying Officers Waghorn and Atcherley, and Flight Lieutenants Stainforth and Greig. The engineering officer was Flying Officer Moon. They moved to Calshot in April using the S.5s for practice.

As usual Mitchell, a rather shy person, felt at home with the RAF contingent, becoming a firm friend of Squadron Leader Orlebar in particular. The team was made welcome to their home by his wife Flo and conversations would last well into the night.

As soon as the first Rolls-Royce 'R' engine arrived at the works it was fitted to the first aircraft and on 5 August Orlebar attempted a test flight. Unfortunately, as had been the case with the S.5, the port float dug in and the aircraft veered to the left due to the torque generated by the 1,900hp engine. Mitchell decided that the solution used on the S.5s might work and fuel was progressively transferred to the starboard float, which was successful. As the maximum speed was increased during the flight tests it became apparent that engine cooling was inadequate. Mitchell increased the area of the surface radiators and arranged for a small airflow through the wings in the radiator positions.

On 6 September the contestants were lined up at Calshot for the Navigability tests. Italy provided the only opposition with two Macchi M.67s (these only had 1,400hp engines) and one Macchi M.52R. The two S.6 aircraft were joined by an S.5 to replace the

Gloster aircraft, which had suffered persistent engine trouble. On completion of these tests the S.6s were plagued by two faults. The first occurred in the water tightness test where the aircraft were moored for several hours. A mechanic noticed that one S.6 was listing and discovered a puncture in a float. Repairs were not allowed so Mitchell was roused from a much-needed sleep. Having studied the list he decided that the aircraft would last for the remaining three hours. He was proved right, although it was a close run thing.

Mitchell was again disturbed from his rest later that night when piston damage was found in one cylinder of the other S.6. However, due to an extremely fortuitous string of events the problem was resolved (see Chapter 2 for the epic story.) A huge crowd of spectators had gathered on the morning of 7 September, including a party of Supermarine workers who had a prime position due to the organization of a pontoon by Mitchell. The race would take place in perfect conditions round a four-sided course of fifty kilometres for seven laps, and Mitchell, as usual, watched proceedings from a launch. Both the Macchi M.67s pulled out on the second lap with engine trouble so the race was contested by the S.6s, the S.5 and the Macchi M.52R. Atcherley in his S.6 was disqualified for cutting a corner and Waghorn won at 328.63mph followed by the Macchi M.52R and the S.5 a close third. However, there was what appeared to be a disastrous finish to the race as far as Waghorn was concerned, as on his last lap his engine started misfiring and finally cut out. He landed safely and no doubt sat there cursing his bad luck, so he was perplexed when the launch arrived with all on board cheering, it turned out that he had miscounted laps (just as Webster did in the 1927 race) and that the failure had occurred on his eighth lap! The cause of the engine shut down was not revealed but, bearing in mind the careful calculation of the minimum fuel required for the race, it may have just been a case of running out of fuel. Cyril Lovesey, exhausted from the labours of the previous night, had to be woken up to hear the result.

The celebrations for this second consecutive win were extensive, including a banquet at the *Savoy Hotel* at which Ramsay MacDonald, the Prime Minster, made a speech in which he congratulated the Italian team for their competitive spirit!

Mitchell was now widely known in the international aviation industry, and there were several offers of employment, which he declined. Rolls-Royce were delighted with the publicity resulting from their participation in the race and supplied Mitchell with cars, the first a rather sombre saloon followed by a yellow coupe and finally, his favourite, a Rolls Bentley.

Apart from the S.6 Mitchell designed an amphibian named the Sea Mew. Powered by two Armstrong Siddeley Jaguar engines, this reconnaissance aircraft resembled a scaled down Southampton. Another design was commissioned by The Hon A.E. Guinness who had been delighted with his Solent flying boat. In a departure from normal practice this had a parasol wing and was powered by three Armstrong Siddeley Jaguar engines. The luxurious accommodation included sleeping quarters. However, it did not meet the specified performance and was sold on, eventually crashing in Italy.

In 1930 Mitchell produced an update of the Southampton, which was designated the Mk X. Once again, he used three Armstrong Siddeley Jaguar engines, with sesquiplane wings and a stainless steel under water part of the hull. The weight of the latter may have caused the poor performance of the aircraft, which did not receive any orders.

The Government gave Supermarine a contract for a large six-engine, forty-passenger, flying boat powered by Rolls-Royce engines; the engine selected is not known but it could have been the Condor or the Buzzard. In the event the depression resulted in the cancellation of this contract, at a late stage in the design process.

Another important member of the team arrived at this time. Beverley Shenstone had been working with the Junkers Company in Germany as an aerodynamics specialist. When he was interviewed he was asked to look at the six-engine project wing by Mitchell. To Mitchell's surprise, Beverley made some critical comments on the design. He was sent away without the offer of a job! Having reviewed the comments, Mitchell realized that Beverley was right and so he became a member of the team who would play a significant role in the design of the Spitfire.

It is perhaps pertinent at this point to reflect on the prolific output of Supermarine designs and with the exception of the Southampton flying boat (eighty-three orders) either small or nil orders at all were made for the rest. It would certainly appear that the involvement of Vickers from 1928 onwards saved this small company from closure.

In January 1931 the Labour Government announced that, due to the Depression, they could not afford to support an entry in the Schneider Trophy. However, as detailed in Chapter 2, Lady Houston came to the rescue with a donation of £100,000. With only seven months to go before the race Mitchell started his design, which would be a modified version of the S.6. The Rolls-Royce 'R' engine would now develop 2,350hp and most of the aircraft changes were aimed at engine cooling. The floats were lengthened to provide more area for the radiators; they also provided the necessary increase in fuel capacity and modifications were made to the oil cooling system. So began a race against time to meet the race deadline.

Two of the S.6B aircraft would be built and the S.6s would incorporate the new floats and engines when they became available. These S.6As would be used for trials, training and as reserves for the race.

The new RAF High Speed Flight with Squadron Leader Orlebar in command once again, consisted of Flight Lieutenants Boothman, Stainforth, Long, Hope and Snaith plus a Fleet Air Arm pilot, Lieutenant Brinton. As soon as the first S.6A became available Orlebar took it up for a test flight, which revealed a problem with tail flutter. Mitchell added mass balances to all moving surfaces and this cured the problem. This modification was applied to all the S.6A and S.6B aircraft. However, the first S.6A with the uprated engine had repetitive problems with spluttering and cut outs. This was traced to fuel filter blockage due to the latest exotic fuel 'brew' provided by F.R. Banks (as detailed in Chapter 2), which was attacking the sealant in the fuel tanks. Mitchell's solution was to keep on flying until the surplus sealant had been removed! When the first S.6B went out for a test flight, Orlebar found that the torque reaction made it impossible to attempt a take-off. Mitchell realized the previous 'fix' of transferring fuel to the starboard float would not be sufficient to overcome the marked increase in torque delivered by the 'R' engine. He therefore experimented with different size propellers and, surprisingly, found that an increase to 9ft 1.5in diameter enabled take-off without serious problems. The photograph of the S.6B shows the aircraft with the new propeller, and although the author feels this may be starting a practice flight, it could be preparation for the victorious, unopposed, 'fly over' flight. Mitchell was presented with yet another problem when the S.6B was found to be unstable in turns. He determined that this was due to the centre of gravity of the aircraft, which was too far aft, and, typically, he came up with the simple solution of reducing the oil tank contents in the extra tank near the fin and putting lead weights in the nose of each float.

These problems must have imposed considerable stress on Mitchell and this was further compounded when, tragically, the Fleet Air Arm pilot, Lieutenant Brinton, was killed when he crashed one of the S.6As whilst attempting his first take-off. With the withdrawal of the French and Italian entries the race would be a walkover for the British. The Royal Aero Club, unlike the Americans, had refused a one-year postponement. In the event Flight Lieutenant Boothman took the S.6B round the triangular course at an average speed of 340.08mph and the Schneider Trophy was now the property of Great Britain in perpetuity. This victory was followed, at the request of Rolls-Royce, by an attempt on the world airspeed record by Flight Lieutenant Stainforth using a 'sprint' version of the 'R' engine developing 2,530hp. He achieved no less than 407.5mph, an impressive performance that would, however, be bettered in 1934 by the Italians when their Macchi MC72 set a new record of 440.7mph. A mark of the close relationship that had evolved between the two companies was that the aircraft was called the Supermarine Rolls-Royce S.6B in press releases. Certainly, the development of the 'R' engine would be a major factor in the production of the Merlin, particularly in the fields of supercharging and materials, equally for Mitchell in the fields of aerodynamics and monococque airframe construction.

126

Once again there were many celebratory dinners, one of which was hosted by the Mayor of Southampton. Mitchell disliked making speeches. But when he did, he always gave an insight to the work involved in preparing for the Schneider Trophy and gave full credit to all those who contributed to the three successes. Mitchell's contribution to the advancement of aviation was recognized in the New Year's Honours list of 1932 with the award of the CBE.

During this year a new recruit to the company, Jack Rasmussen, who had worked for the Blackburn Aircraft Company, joined Mitchell's team, initially as a draughtsman but later took charge of design liaison for Supermarine. Reverting to 'Bread and Butter' aircraft Mitchell designed an upgrade of the Southampton flying boat originally designated Southampton IV, later changed to Scapa. This was powered by two Rolls-Royce Kestrel engines and featured an enclosed cockpit and a larger hull than its predecessor. It had a top speed of 142mph and a range of 1,100 miles. The RAF ordered fifteen Scapas.

Mitchell now started to consider a fighter design to meet with the rather unambitious specification F7/30 issued by the Air Ministry in 1930. The salient features were a maximum speed of 250mph, good visibility, and a high initial rate of climb and armament of four 0.303 machine guns.

However, he was not finished with his biplane designs; first came an amphibian that was to find fame as the Walrus, although it started life as the Seagull V. This aircraft was originally ordered by the Australian Air Force for catapult launch from cruisers. It was capable of launch with a full complement of armaments consisting of three 0.303 machine guns and 760lb of bombs or depth-charges plus a crew of three. It was powered by a 750hp Bristol Pegasus in pusher configuration, having a maximum speed of 135mph and a range of 600 miles. Designed to be suitable for catapult launch from warships and with folding wings and an enclosed cockpit, it was aimed at naval use. Initially, the Walrus did not generate much interest in the UK services. However, in 1935 an order from the Air Ministry for fifteen aircraft was received, and eventually the total production was 760 Seagull V and Walrus Mk 1 and Mk 2 variants.

It was operated by the RAF, RAAF, RNZAF, RCAF and RZNF. It was renowned in the Second World War for its amazing exploits in the Air/Sea Rescue role, and it was one of Mitchell's most outstanding successes.

Mitchell designed a follow-up to the Walrus known as the Sea Otter. This amphibian was powered by a 965hp Bristol Mercury engine mounted in a tractor configuration. It had a maximum speed of 163mph and a range of 920 miles. The first flight took place in 1938 but it did not enter service with the RAF and RN until 1944. A total of 292 Sea Otters were produced.

Mitchell's final flying boat design was the Stranraer, an improved version of the Scapa. Powered by two Pegasus X engines of 920hp, it had a maximum speed of 165mph and a range of 1,000 miles. The first flight took place in 1934 and it entered RAF service in 1937. Seventeen aircraft were built at Supermarine and a further forty by the Canadian Vickers Company. Operated by the RAF and the RCAF in the coastal patrol role, they completed their military service in 1942. Thirteen aircraft were converted for commercial use by three Canadian operators with the last operation occurring in 1957.

Mitchell now turned his attention to the fighter aircraft covered by the 1930 Specification F7/30. Allocated the type number 224, this was to be one of Mitchell's failures. A low (cranked to keep the fixed undercarriage as short as possible) wing monoplane, with an open cockpit and powered by a Rolls-Royce Goshawk engine of 600hp failed to meet the performance requirements. The Goshawk relied on steam cooling where the water was circulated under pressure in the engine and then emitted as steam into condensers. This was thought to give a more efficient temperature reduction than radiators and since the condensers could be built into the leading edges of the Type 224, removed the drag associated with radiators. Mitchell had started on modifications resulting in a similar aircraft to the Hurricane but Sir Robert McLean instructed him to give up on the 224 and start afresh on a 'real killer fighter'.

Mitchell had been feeling tired and, seeking advice, received the shocking news that he had rectal cancer. He underwent an immediate colostomy (as had Henry Royce). After convalescence he returned to work and managed to conceal his condition from most of his colleagues.

The Air Ministry had refused to issue a new fighter specification so Sir Robert contacted Arthur Sidgreaves at Rolls-Royce and it was agreed that their PV12 engine and the new Supermarine design (type 300) would proceed as private ventures. The Air Ministry was informed of this decision and advised that interference with the two projects would not be countenanced! At the same time Rolls-Royce donated £7,500 towards the construction of the type 300 proto-type. This resulted in a rapid 'volte-face' by the Ministry within one month, with contracts given to both companies and the issue of a new specification, F37/34. Mitchell, conscious of the possibility that his cancer could well return, embarked with his team on a period of high activity. However, Mitchell did find time to take flying lessons, starting in December 1934 and gaining his pilot's licence in July 1935. He also continued to play golf with some tournament success.

After several preliminary sketches the familiar shape began to emerge. Mitchell and Shenstone spent many hours on the wing design. Based on his Schneider experience Mitchell wanted to keep the wing as thin as possible (contrary to the accepted practice of a thick wing for lift) consistent with sufficient thickness from the root to accommodate the retracting undercarriage and the machine guns (only four specified at this time). It was Shenstone who suggested the elliptical shape and Mitchell accepted this and the slight 'wash out' to the wing form with +2 degrees incidence at the root taper-ing to −½ degree at the tip, which had a significant effect on aero-dynamic performance, in particular reducing tip stall, which could lead to a spin. When the design was finalized Joe Smith was respon-sible for final approval of all the detail drawings.

The main fuselage consisted of fifteen oval frames connected by stringers and longerons clad in riveted aluminium sheet varying from 18swg (standard wire gauge) at the front to 22swg at the tail end. The tail section and fin were constructed of frames covered in 24swg aluminium and the tailplanes had front and rear spars and ribs covered with aluminium. The elevators and rudder consisted of frames with Irish linen covering.

129

Since the Merlin was to use the evaporative steam cooling system the wing featured the D section leading edge section for the condensers. This was light but very strong and it was retained when the Merlin changed to glycol cooling; in later models it was adopted for extra fuel tankage. The wing section was based on the NACA 2200 series adapted to give a thickness/chord ratio of 13 per cent at the root, reducing to 6 per cent at the tip. An innovative spar boom design involved five square tubes that fitted into each other; these were progressively cut away to match the thinning of the wing. Two of these booms linked together by an aluminium web structure, resulting in a lightweight, very strong, main spar. The covering was aluminium sheet of 14swg at the leading edge and 24swg for the rest of the wing; flush riveting was used for the crucial aerodynamic areas. The ailerons were covered in Irish linen due to the concern that metal covering would produce heavy loads for the pilot in violent manoeuvres. There were no trim tabs on the ailerons and trim adjustments were achieved by bending their trailing edges! The undercarriage configuration with the mounting points inboard of the wheel location gave a narrow track that was not too popular with pilots. Mitchell was concerned that putting the mounting points outboard (as with the Hurricane) would put too much stress on the thin wing. Another effect was that with the change to eight machine guns there was quite a spread between the guns compared with the close positioning of the Hurricane guns. This change was originated by Squadron Leader Ralph Sorley who had calculated that with the relative speeds of modern bombers and fighter aircraft the latter would have a two-second period of holding the enemy in the gunsight, and that it would be necessary to provide interceptors with six or preferably eight 0.303 calibre machine guns. This was covered by specification F10/35. This did cause Mitchell some problems as the wing design catered for four guns and the extra guns would be in the thinner section of the wings so it was difficult to accommodate them and their ammunition boxes.

Based at the Air Ministry, Sorley had access to senior personnel and went on to recommend that both the Supermarine and Hawker aircraft be put into production as soon as possible, with the Gloster

Gladiator four-gun biplane production order being cancelled. His recommendation was accepted, although there were still misgivings about monoplanes so the Gladiator production order was retained!

Frederick Meredith of Farnborough produced a very efficient design for the under wing-mounted radiator duct, which actually produced thrust; not enough to eliminate the duct drag but certainly a useful reduction. It would become evident later that the complexity of the wing, in particular the close tolerances required on the spar booms, would be the principal cause of production delays. In the meantime Mitchell designed a version of the type 300 for the turret fighter specification F9/35; fortunately this lost out to the Boulton Paul Defiant design.

The initial target for the first flight, of the now officially named Spitfire (to Mitchell's disgust), was scheduled for January 1936. Vickers said, subject to an order being placed on 1 May, this would enable them to start production in September 1936 at the rate of five aircraft per week. However, a series of delays completely destroyed this over-optimistic forecast and caused considerable concern for the Air Ministry.

The prototype K5054 with Mutt Summers at the controls took off from Eastleigh on 6 March 1936. Fitted with a fine pitch two-blade propeller, the take-off run was very short. The flight with the undercarriage locked down lasted for twenty minutes. On landing Mutt said 'Do not touch anything.' This did not mean that he felt the aircraft was perfect, rather that he wanted to maintain the configuration as a datum for the following test flights. For the following flights the undercarriage doors and a coarse pitch propeller were fitted for maximum speed tests. The only major problem during the tests was that the rudder horn balance was too large, resulting in unacceptably light operation and directional instability at high speed. The maximum speed was disappointing – well short of 350mph. There were modifications in hand to cater for these problems. On 10 April K5054 was hangared for modifications. The balance horn size was reduced; the top of the rudder squared off; the carburettor intake lowered and the top engine cowling strengthened. Via the Rolls-Royce car division their sub contract car painting specialists were enlisted to paint the aircraft. This involved four days of repeated filling of gaps and rubbing down before the final coat of blue-grey paint was applied.

Flight testing resumed and it was found that with the 950hp Merlin C engine the maximum speed was only 335mph. This caused consternation, 'Would the Air Ministry order a complex aircraft that was no faster that the relatively simple Hurricane?' Investigation revealed that the propeller tips were running into Mach problems. A new propeller was designed and, to relief all round, a speed of 348mph was obtained.

The aircraft was now handed over to the RAF at Martlesham, and the first pilot to sample it was Flight Lieutenant Edward-Jones. He found it a delight to fly but only remembered to lower the under-carriage at the last moment. With the cockpit open for the approach and with his helmet on, the warning horn was drowned out by the engine noise. He suggested an undercarriage position indicator on the control panel. In the event a louder horn positioned just behind the pilot's head proved sufficient. Based on his report the Air Ministry placed a contract for 310 Spitfires on 3 June 1936.

Test flights continued with Jeffrey Quill and RAF pilots carrying out the programme. However, first there were modifications to be installed. On 19 September work started in preparation for the installation of the eight Browning machine guns and, at the same time, the new Merlin F was installed. This engine gave improved performance of 1,050hp at an altitude of 16,000ft. Quill's first test flights on 3 December were checks on the oil cooler efficiency at varying speeds and power settings. On 10 December performance flights with a fixed-pitch four-bladed propeller showed no improve-ment over the two-blade version. His next test involved spins and for this he was provided with a spin recovery parachute; this crude manual system gave Quill some concern as he had to deploy it from the cockpit left handed and on a right-hand spin the wire would pass perilously near to his throat. In the event this device was not needed as the Spitfire behaved in exemplary fashion.

Early in 1937 an extraordinary series of tests took place to check the benefits of flush riveting, which was more time consuming in production than normal dome head snap riveting The latter was reproduced by gluing half peas on all the wing and front and rear fuselage flush rivets with Seccotine (a well-known adhesive in my carpentry days at school). The results of a series of tests removing peas from specific areas showed a total loss of 22mph. Flush riveting was retained!

The next series of tests, instigated by the Air Ministry, involved tail-wheels of dual and single wheel configuration; the latter being selected. Mitchell could not understand why the tail skid needed to be replaced. Amazingly, the Ministry did not tell him (on the grounds of secrecy), that they were planning hard surface runways for the front-line airfields, which would wear out skids. It was also found that the flow rate of the standard RAF fuel bowsers was too high for the connecting pipe between the upper and lower fuel tanks. Finally, on 10 March gun-firing tests commenced and it was found that at 32,000ft the guns tended to jam due to the ambient temperature of $-53°C$. Another fault, connected with the gun breeches having to be left open, occurred when a hard landing by the RAF pilot resulted in three of the guns firing a single shot each in the direction of Felixstowe!

On 21 March K5054 suffered her first accident. Flying Officer McKenna had been testing a revised gearing of the stick to elevators. This involved a series of loops culminating in a 4g effort, when the Merlin failed as the aircraft g dropped towards normal. He made a dead stick landing, undercarriage up, in a field. Fortunately, the two-blade propeller had stopped in the horizontal position so the damage was relatively slight.

From early 1937 Mitchell's health deteriorated to the extent that he made fewer visits to the design office. An exploratory operation revealed that the cancer had returned and was not treatable. He died on 11 June at the age of forty-two, a great shock to his colleagues as right up to the end he had concealed the extent of his illness. It was a tremendous loss to the aviation industry, and who knows what he would have achieved if he been able to continue pushing the boundaries of technology. His last design was a heavy bomber to specification B 12/36. This featured a monocoque fuselage, and the wing had a swept back leading edge (Shenstone's influence perhaps). Powered by four Merlins it was estimated that this aircraft would have a maximum speed of 360mph. Two prototypes were commissioned, but these were destroyed in a bombing raid on the Supermarine factory at Woolston, Southampton, in September 1940 and the project was abandoned, a telling blow by the *Luftwaffe*.

Like Royce, Mitchell had left behind an excellent team and Joe Smith, promoted to chief designer, would oversee the continued development of the Spitfire. On 19 September a speed test with the ejector exhausts (see Chapter 2) gave a true airspeed of 360mph. Lengthy trials of a series of modifications to overcome the problem of gun failure at high altitudes, particularly the outer guns in the port wing, came to a satisfactory conclusion on 6 October. The main changes were ducting the exhaust of the radiator to both wings and a bulkhead in the port wing outboard of the wheel bay. K5054 continued to explore the flight envelope and test in-service modifications, suffering two landing accidents in night flying tests, One of these was caused by the failure of flaps and brakes due to lack of air pressure. A larger air compressor was fitted and flying continued until 4 September 1939 when an RAF pilot stalled her on final approach, finishing up inverted. The pilot suffered fatal injuries and the decision was taken to scrap the aircraft. Thus ended an invaluable test programme involving over 100 flying hours.

As a result of input from RAF pilots the Air Ministry requested changes for production Spitfires. The current maximum diving speed of 380mph, limited due to wing flutter, was to be increased to 450mph. This was achieved by moving the wing spar web structure, linking the two spar booms from front to rear of the booms and applying a heavier gauge alloy covering to the D-section leading edge. A dive speed of 470mph was achieved by Jeffery Quill who noted that aileron control became very heavy. He later remarked that he wished he had realized the significance of this.

Other changes were to increase the fuel tank capacity from 75 to 85 gallons and to increase the flap travel from 57 to 85 degrees. In addition, changes to ease production would involve Joe Smith and his team changing the majority of the production drawings, which would require an estimated total of one year's work. The revised target of October 1937 for the delivery of the first aircraft to the RAF would be adversely effected, in part due to delays in the availability of these drawings.

It became quite obvious to the Air Ministry that the Supermarine factory was too small to handle the Spitfire production programme as well as a large order for the Walrus amphibian. Sir Robert Mclean was loath to release their technology to other companies but Air Ministry pressure forced him to subcontract the tail assembly production to General Aviation. However, this action did not help as delays continued due to wing production falling behind the rest of the airframe components. Finally, it was agreed that four-fifths of the components would be subcontracted, and this resulted in the first aircraft being delivered to 19 Squadron in July 1938. It was realized that it was essential to boost the production rate and to this end, in 1938, the Air Ministry commissioned a large new factory at Castle Bromwich, to be run by the Morris Motor Company; the production would be exclusively the Spitfire Mk II. This got off to a disastrous start with Lord Nuffield trying to use car production techniques and by 17 May 1940 not a single aircraft had been delivered. Lord Beaverbrook who had recently been appointed as Minister of Aircraft Production decided to hand the factory over to Vickers, which resulted in an increase in production from twenty-three in July to fifty-six in September. 611 Squadron received the first Mk II in August so there were a limited number of these aircraft available for the Battle of Britain.

The first sixty Spitfire Mk I production aircraft did not have the gun heating modification, and this could not be retro-fitted until successful trials had been completed by K5054. The two-blade wooden propeller was fitted to the first seventy-seven aircraft; thereafter the three-blade de Havilland or Rotol propellers were fitted. Rotol was a new company jointly owned by Rolls-Royce and Bristol. These manufacturers would supply three- and four-bladed constant speed propellers. Early RAF experience confirmed the need for some design changes that had been reported by the Supermarine test pilots and modifications were in the course of preparation. The main changes were a bulged canopy to give more headroom; hydraulic operation of the undercarriage; and a higher speed starter motor.

At the outbreak of war, on 3 September 1939, there were 306 Spitfires with RAF Squadrons 19, 41, 54, 65, 66, 72, 74, 602, 603 and 611 (the last three were RAF Auxiliary Squadrons). 602 City of Glasgow and 603 City of Edinburgh Squadrons were involved in the first action of the war over mainland Britain on 16 October, when they repelled an attack by Ju 88s on warships moored at Rosyth on the Firth of Forth, each Squadron shooting down one aircraft.

By the onset of the Battle of Britain there were a total of nineteen operational Spitfire squadrons and the aircraft had undergone a number of modifications The Battle of Britain has been covered elsewhere, but there are one or two interesting Spitfire events. One of these, on 23 January 1940, involved the first action of a prototype Mk I armed with two 20mm Hispano cannon but no machine guns, a mistake as it turned out in this action. Pilot Officer George Proudman joined a flight of Hurricanes who were directed to a lone Heinkel 111. However, they were beaten to it by three 602 Squadron Spitfires, who were carrying out a series of attacks. As they broke off Proudman closed in and opened fire. One high-explosive round was fired by the port gun before it had a stoppage; this knocked a piece off the port wing of the Heinkel, and the starboard gun fired thirty ball rounds before it too suffered a stoppage. The 602 Squadron Spitfires finished off the attack. It is interesting that two types of 20mm ammunition were being evaluated at this time. The cause of the stoppage problem was the lack of rigidity of the cannon mounting and the need to cant the gun on its side, resulting in problems with the cartridge belt feed and ejection system. Nevertheless, it was recognized that the cannon were very effective weapons and that they should be accompanied by four 0.303 machine guns. With modified installations the cannon-equipped Spitfires were identified as Mk IB and IIB respectively. However, their deployment was initially delayed until the four machine gun versions were available, and this took place in November 1940, after the conclusion of the Battle of Britain.

Another event, in August and September 1940, was the award of an RAF temporary commission to enable Jeffery Quill to take part in combat actions. During this time he shot down an Me109 and had a share in a Heinkel 1-11. More importantly, he came back with several recommendations to improve the Spitfire's fighting ability. The most urgent of these was the problem of the ailerons locking almost solid in a high-speed dive. This was traced to the fabric covering ballooning and replacement of the fabric with light alloy provided a complete cure, as confirmed by Squadron Leader Sandy Johnstone of 602 Squadron when he flew the first modified aircraft. Quill also recommended changes to the cockpit canopy to improve forward and rearward visibility; in the latter case his suggestion of a teardrop canopy with a cut down rear fuselage was not adopted until much later. He also asked for improvements in the jettisoning of the canopy due to cases of pilots becoming trapped in the cockpit when attempting to bale out.

By mid-1940 the Spitfire had been subject to a number of changes, mainly as a result of RAF experience, 73lb of armour plating being added to protect the pilot, the addition of an IFF (Identity Friend or Foe) aerial for transmission of an identifying signal to reduce the number of 'friendly fire' losses; an armoured glass panel in front of the windscreen and a thicker duralumin sheet for the top engine cowling. The increased weight and drag associated with these changes resulted in a significant reduction in maximum speed to 350mph.

The advent of 100 octane fuel in the spring of 1940 allowed the Merlin's boost to be increased to 12psi, giving a marked increase of 34mph at 10,000ft. However, at higher altitudes the single-stage single speed supercharger limited the effect of the boost increase. A small gain in speed was achieved by moving the armoured glass panel to the inside of the windscreen, improving it by about 6mph. At an altitude of 17,500ft the maximum speed was 354mph, not much of an increase in what was the realm of action. The Spitfire Mk II that entered service in August 1940 had a very similar performance.

Prior to the outbreak of war Sydney Cotton had taken clandestine aerial photographs of Italian fortifications in Libya from a Lockheed 12 transport aircraft. Flying Officer Longbottom suggested that this role might be filled by a single-engine fighter. Initially, his advice was ignored and a twin-engine Blenheim was modified for the role. It was not a success. With the outbreak of war Cotton was appointed Wing Commander in charge of the Photographic Development unit with Longbottom as one of his pilots and design experts. Two Spitfire Mk I aircraft were provided and these had the armament removed and the gun ports covered by metal strips. Two cameras were fitted in the wings and extensive filling and polishing of the airframe was undertaken by the 'Speed Spitfire' experts at Heston. All this gave a maximum speed increase of about 15mph, judged to be sufficient to outrun any opposition. One aircraft piloted by Longbottom was stationed in France and carried out the first photo reconnaissance sorties in November 1939. These flights revealed that photographs from 30,000ft with the 5-inch focal length cameras did not give sufficient detail of troop and transport movements. Cotton obtained 8-inch focal length cameras to give some improvement but the decision was taken to move to low-level flights over targets. The other problem was the lack of range of the Spitfire. This was tackled in stages by fitting slipper tanks under the wings; fitting a 29-gallon tank behind the cockpit; and converting the D-section leading edge in each wing to hold 57 gallons of fuel (later increased to 63.5 gallons), giving a maximum range of 1,800 miles, The Mark number of each variant was identified by a prefix and suffix, from PR Mk IA through to PR Mk IG. Lower-level flights with oblique cameras were dangerous but very successful as in the case of Pilot Officer Green's photograph of Brest harbour in April 1941, which showed the battle cruisers *Scharnhorst* and *Gneisenau* in dock. Later photo reconnaissance variants included the Mk IV.

A deviation from the Spitfire's original role was air-sea rescue, which started in 1943 using Mk II aircraft that had been replaced in service and was achieved without modification to the airframe. The dinghy and survival canisters were contained in the flare chutes behind the Spitfire's cockpit.

Another new role was that of a fighter floatplane, this high priority programme was initiated in April 1940 with the onset of the Norway campaign and applied to the Spitfire and Hurricane. The floats used, taken from the Blackburn Roc, were too large and too heavy but time did not permit development of new floats. The project was dropped after the end of the Norway campaign, but resurrected in 1942 for potential operation in the Pacific. A prototype based on the Spitfire Mk V with floats designed by Arthur Shirvall of Supermarine, who had designed the floats for the Schneider Trophy machines, was first flown by Quill in October 1942. In February 1943 it was shipped to Helensburgh, Scotland, where it was joined by two more produced by Folland Aircraft, for service trials. Possible use in the Mediterranean Dodecanese islands was forestalled by the German occupation of these islands. The final attempt was based on the Mk IX for potential use in the Pacific, and this sole conversion had a useful maximum speed of about 360mph at low altitude, and handled well in the trials, however the programme was cancelled.

We should mention the 'Speed Spitfire', a rather special Mk I prepared for an attempt on the world landplane speed record held by Howard Hughes at 325mph.

Hughes took due cognisance of the the Italian Macchi floatplane's outright record of 441mph, but naturally Hollywood ignored this in their film of his life! The modifications involved removing all surplus equipment such as armament, radio etc.; wing span reduction to 28ft with rounded tips; fairing over access panels; full flush riveting; the 'Speed Merlin' engine (see Chapter 2); a wooden four-blade coarse pitch propeller and a streamlined cockpit canopy. A great deal of filler was applied to all joints and seams, with much polishing and a high gloss paint finish. While all this was going on the German Bf109 had set a new record of 379mph followed by the He100 at 394mph. The first flights of the 'Speed Spitfire' gave an estimated 400mph at the record attempt altitude of 200ft. The decision was taken to delete the large radiator entirely and use a 'boiling' tank, to give an estimated 425mph. However, the He100 took the world airspeed record at 463mph followed by the Me209 at 469mph, well out of reach for the 'Speed Spitfire'. The aircraft was returned to a useful configuration with the installation of a Merlin XII engine; a three-blade propeller, and the radiators were reinstated. In this form it was still a fast aircraft so it was delivered to the fledgling reconnaissance squadron, in November 1940. Fitted with an oblique camera it was chosen for the low-level role. However, its range was such that on a sortie to Brest it would have ditched in the Channel on its return flight! It continued as a station runabout until it was scrapped in 1946.

There were a number of wing forms designed for different Marks of Spitfires. These included the Type A, which was the original wing with eight 0.303 machine guns; the Type B designed for two 20mm cannon and four 0.303 machine guns; the Type C, a universal wing that could accept either A and B armament or four 20mm cannon; the Type D, an unarmed wing for photo reconnaissance aircraft with the D-shaped leading edge adapted for fuel tanks; and the Type E for a rearranged weapon position with two 20mm cannon outboard of two 0.50 machine guns or four cannon. This wing was introduced on Mk IX and XVI Spitfires; it also had the capability of carrying two 250lb bombs.

Twenty two-seat Spitfires were produced for training purposes; based on surplus aircraft the main modification involved moving the cockpit forward to allow for the second cockpit, which featured a full set of controls and instrumentation. Some carried armament, usually four 0.303 machine guns. A two-seat Spitfire very much in current use is the Grace Spitfire. This aircraft, which had been converted to two-seat configuration after the Second World War by Supermarine for the Irish Air Corps, was rebuilt by Nick Grace over a five-year period culminating in a first flight in 1985. Tragically, Nick was killed in a road accident in 1988; his widow, Caroline, learned to fly the Spitfire and today it is one of the most active Spitfires on the aviation show circuit.

The Sea Spitfire, quickly named the Seafire, resulted from an Admiralty request for a carrier borne version of the Spitfire Mk I. The initial requests were rejected as apparently Winston Churchill thought the Fairey Fulmar would suffice. However, the request was finally accepted as the Fleet Air Arm saw the need for a counter to the Japanese Zero fighter. Basic changes consisted of a strengthened rear fuselage, folding wings and an arrester hook. Although the original aircraft's narrow track, rather frail undercarriage plus propeller torque reaction caused many problems on take-off and land-on, a total of 2,336 were produced, progressively overcoming these deficiencies. The ultimate Seafire was the Griffon-powered Mk 47 with Rotol contra-rotating propellers. This must have been a most welcome change for the pilots from the very considerable torque reaction on the other Griffon Seafires. Other improvements were hydraulic wing folding, a lowered rear fuselage and a teardrop cockpit canopy. They saw action in the Malaysian emergency and the early days of the Korean War. All Seafires were withdrawn from Royal Navy service in 1951.

We can say that the Spitfire was a very versatile aircraft that was developed, along with the Rolls-Royce Merlin and Griffon engines, throughout the Second World War to match or exceed the perform-ance of the opposing *Luftwaffe* piston engine aircraft.

Including the Seafire, there were a total of thirty-five different Mark numbers. This figure provides a measure of the tremendous workload on Joe Smith and his team. Spitfires were operated by the air forces of no fewer than thirty-six countries in nearly every theatre of the Second World War. The last operational Spitfire, a two-seat trainer, was removed from service in 1961 with the Irish Air Corps. There are about forty-four airworthy Spitfires today out of the total production of 20,351.

A comparison between the Mk I and the final version, the Spitfire Mk 24, shows the astonishing changes achieved in performance in something like eight years:

	Spitfire Mk 1	Spitfire Mk 24
Wing span	36ft 10in	36ft 11in
Length	29ft 11in	32ft 11in
Weight (loaded)	5,700lb	9,900lb
Power plant	Merlin Mk II, 27 litre 1,030hp	Griffon Mk 61, 37 litre 2,035hp
Max. speed	350mph @ 18,500ft	460mph @ 26,000ft

	Spitfire Mk 1	Spitfire Mk 24
Rate of climb	2,300ft/min	4,880ft/min
Service ceiling	36,000ft	43,000ft
Range (internal tanks)	780 miles	860 miles
Armament	8 × 0.303 machine guns	4 × 20mm cannon
Provision for		three 500lb bombs, or Rocket launchers, or two drop tanks

Those pilots who survived to fly the various marks of Spitfire throughout the war tended to regard the Mk V and the Mk IX (a Mk V modified to take the Merlin 65) as their all-round favourites in combat action and the Mk II as the easiest to fly – 'it seemed to respond to changes of attitude as soon as you thought about it'. A brief summary of their attributes follows:

	Mk V	Mk IX
Max speed (mph)	371 @ 20,000ft	405 @ 28,000 ft
Rate of climb (approx.)	3,350ft/min	4,000ft/min
Service ceiling	37,500ft	43,100ft

I well remember my father arriving home exhausted in the summer of 1944 after a fifteen-hour overnight drive from RAF stations in the south. He had been adjusting the boost to 25lb on Spitfire Mk IX aircraft, made possible by the use of 150 octane fuel. The resulting extra 30mph at lower altitude enabled the pilots to catch the V-1 'Doodlebugs'. The pilots were not so enamoured of the need to go to full throttle every ten minutes in cruise to clear the spark plugs of lead build up.

The Spitfire was the only Allied aircraft in continuous production throughout the war. The fact that it could be upgraded to match the performance of the developing Bf109 variants and the new FW190 says a great deal about Mitchell's original design. He did see the prototype fly, unlike Royce who did not live to see the Merlin run. Nevertheless, like Royce he had built up an extremely able team with the inspired leadership of chief designer Joe Smith who developed his design so effectively.

We should also mention the Spiteful, Joe Smith's last piston-engine design. He had recognized the problem of compressibility, which limited the Spitfire to a maximum speed (in a dive) of 480mph due to flexing of the wing behind the stiff leading edge. Its pilot was a brave man with not an ejection seat to be seen! In 1942 he started work on a laminar flow wing, which he also tailored for ease of production. This was received well by the Air Ministry who issued Specification 1/43 in February 1943. The first flight took place on 30 June 1944. The design was based on a modified Spitfire Mk V fuselage and a welcome change for the pilots was the substitution of a wide-track inward-folding undercarriage. The power plant was the R-R Griffon 85 of 2,375hp. An order was placed for 150 aircraft, later cancelled due to the advent of the Meteor and Vampire jet fighters. An aircraft carrier-based version named the Seafang was developed, featuring contra-rotating propellers and folding wings, but again with the successful carrier operational trials of the Sea Vampire this requirement was dropped. A total of twenty-two Spitefuls and eighteen Seafangs were produced; one of the Spitefuls fitted with a Griffon 101 of 2,420hp achieved a speed of 494mph. The Spiteful wing design was used in Joe Smith's first jet-powered fighter, the Attacker.

Chapter 5

The German Terror Weapons

The V-1

On 17 August 1943, 324 Merlin-engined Lancaster bombers were part of the RAF force bombing Peenemünde, the research centre for the V-1 flying bomb and V-2 rocket. The Germans were nearly ready with these countermeasures to reverse their defeat.

This all started when the *Luftwaffe* developed the V-1 at Peenemünde where its first flight took place at the end of 1941. Our Intelligence knew about it by the end of 1942, leading up to Operation *Crossbow*. This combined the efforts of RAF high altitude (30,000ft) photo reconnaissance, with spy reports, which showed that launching ramps were targeted on London. The data were analysed from photos with 60 per cent overlap to show height changes in 3D, and shadows that gave a complete picture of a V-1 ramp or a vertically pointing V-2. This needed high intelligence and the best vision. The RAF claimed they could even see a man on a bicycle; there was little in Germany they didn't see. Data on the V-1 came from several sources. At RAF Medmenham, a sharp-eyed WAAF officer, Constance Babington-Smith, saw a tiny aircraft in one photo of a railed ramp aimed out to sea at Peenemünde. The Polish Home Army also provided major intelligence on V-1 construction and Peenemünde. In France an agent, Michel Hollard, checked a large concrete installation near Rouen, got a job on site and found a ramp pointed in London's direction. Hollard cycled around northern France and found other structures being built. He even got plans for the Bois Carré site, close to one of the First World War cemeteries at Vimy Ridge, five miles north of Arras. When this information reached the Chief of Staff, General Ismay, he sent the following report to Churchill:

> The Chief-of-Staff feels that you should be made aware of reports of German experiments with long-range rockets. Five reports received since the end of 1942 indicate this fact even if details are inaccurate. We should not lose time in confirming the facts, and must devise counter measures. We suggest you should appoint Duncan Sandys to investigate. It is not considered desirable to inform the public at this stage, when the evidence is so intangible.

Churchill then appointed Duncan Sandys as fact finder, who soon told him about German experiments with jet-propelled planes, heavy rockets, and airborne rocket torpedoes at Peenemünde. Installations were also identified in northern France. In June 1943, Sandys told Churchill that more had been found out about rockets and flying bombs. He advised Churchill to order Bomber Command to attack Peenemünde as soon as possible, and the raid immediately took place. The Home Office set up the evacuation of children and pregnant women. More Morrison shelters, last seen in the Blitz, were also supplied to London.

Robert Lusser of Fieseler designed the 4,750lb V-1. Its Amatol warhead in the nose weighed 1,870lb. Its fuselage was simply made of welded sheet steel, and it had steel or plywood wings, set mid-wing at 35 per cent of its length. A short pylon at the rear of the fuselage took the front of its single motor, and the top of its fin supported the back.

Fritz Gosslau designed its motor, the Argus pulsejet. This was a tube with a flap valve at the front. Ignition or motor heat set off injected fuel, and the bang closed the valve. Pressure increase in the tube forced the gases out at the rear (cylindrical for the last third of its length) giving the motor its thrust. It ran at 40 to 50 pulses per second, making the typical V-1 noise that we recall so well, like a badly adjusted and fast-running railway diesel, and terrifying to those who heard it. I can hear it still! Aldershot folk hated it as RAE Farnborough tested a captured one; the noise was awful and they

146

didn't know what was going on. Londoners always asked a V-1 to keep going, as they knew it would dive to earth and explode when its motor died. Even with all that destruction and death, the citizens of Croydon, with their black sense of humour, called it the 'Doodlebug'.

The pulsejet did not need forward speed for its operation, due to the clever design of its intake vane system and acoustically tuned resonant combustion chamber. V-1 film footage confirmed this as it showed the distinctive pulsating jet exhaust of the motor before the launch system was triggered. A compressed air line started the motor with the V-1 stationary on its ramp. The motor's low static thrust and the high stalling speed of its small wings did not give it enough flying speed for a short take off. So either a modified Heinkel He1-11 or a ground ramp gave it the 360mph flying speed required.

A simple autopilot controlled its flying height and speed. A weighted pendulum system gave it fore-and-aft attitude. Its gyro-compass was set by 'swinging' the V-1 in a hangar before launch and controlled both pitch and roll. It was angled above the horizontal so that interaction between yaw, roll, and other sensors needed only rudder control.

Trim was critical, proved when a V-1 landed intact in March 1945 between Tilburg and Goirle in Holland. Six issues of the German magazine *Signal* were found stuffed in the left wing's tubular steel spar, to balance its static equilibrium before launching. The first V-1s were fitted with a small radio transmitting flight direction between the launch site and the target from the V-1 radio bearing.

A vane on the nose drove an odometer to tell when the target area had been reached, and this was accurate enough for area bombing. A counter was set before launch, allowing for wind speed, and ran down to zero at the target. As the V-1 flew, airflow turned the vane. Thirty turns reduced the count by one. To keep straying V-1s away from launch sites the counter armed the warhead after forty miles from launch, academic as it would explode on impact anyway. The counter set the distance it travelled from its launch on a ramp pointing in the target's direction. When the count fell to zero, two detonating bolts were fired, releasing elevator spoilers, and jamming the linkage between the elevator and servo. A guillotine then cut the rudder servo control hoses, centring the rudder. This put the V-1 into a 45-degree dive, originally intended to be a power dive, but the g force stopped fuel flow, and the motor cut. The fuel problem was quickly fixed, and the last V-1s hit targets at full power – with no warning.

The V-1 and its motor had the following specifications:

V-1 specifications

V-1		Pulse jet	
Airframe	Fieseler Fi 103	Pulse jet motor	Argus As 109-014
Length	27 feet 4 inches	Length	144 inches
Width	17 feet 6 inches	Maximum diameter	22 inches
Height	4 feet 8 inches	Tailpipe diameter	15 inches
Range	150 miles	Tailpipe length	69 inches
Speed	393 mph at 2,000 to 3,000 ft	Weight	344lb
Control	Gyrocompass and autopilot	Static thrust	500lb
		Max thrust	800lb

Intelligence gained prior to the raid on Peenemünde, the zoning of fighters and good ack-ack gun-laying with their new proximity fuses, destroyed many V-1s before launch, or shot them down before they reached our cities. In their zone, the RAF used the best fighters, the Spitfires and the Tempests, to shoot down V-1s, nudge them off course, or tumble their gyros by flipping them over with a wingtip under the wing – a daring but successful manoeuvre. Shooting them down was dangerous as the explosion filled the sky. Pilots had no choice but to fly through a vast cloud of erupting debris.

The papers warned us about these two awful weapons before their arrival. The V-1 could destroy an acre of property. The first V-1 struck London close to the Grove Road railway bridge in Mile End, killing eight civilians on 13 June 1944. Others hit Swanscombe and Sevenoaks in Kent, Cuckfield in Sussex, and Bethnal Green in London. V-1s indiscriminately caused both civilian and service casualties. On 18 June, a V-1 hit the Guard's Chapel at Wellington barracks, killing 121 people and wounding sixty-eight others. By the end of June, 500 V-1s had been fired, and by 5 July 2,500 people had been killed. Even the Air Ministry in the Strand had been hit with the death of 198 people.

The last V-1 struck Datchworth in Hertfordshire on 29 March 1945.

The V-2

The mastermind behind the V-2 was Walter Dornberger, and the brain behind it was Wernher von Braun. Both the V-1 and V-2 were made by forced labour, in cruel conditions of extreme slavery. The V-2 was developed from basics in the 1930s, but operationally followed the V-1, and was the last German weapon to hit British cities. It did a lot of damage for its size, as it was no taller than a three-storey tenement and nothing near the size of a space rocket of today. It was driven by a motor double the size of an AGA cooker. The College of Aeronautics at Cranfield was given one, bent and buckled but relatively intact. The only way the RAF could defeat the V-2 was to destroy its factories, transport and launch sites. To counter RAF attention, desperate German crews even launched V-2s from mobile launchers quickly set up in wooded Dutch suburbs, which provided both good approach roads and excellent camouflage. We could not stop a V-2 once it was in flight. This weapon nearly caused us a government crisis. In addition to the damage, death and injury the V-1 and V-2 caused, there was a psychological element to their menace; the V-1 as it was pilot-less; and the V-2 because it arrived quietly before it blew up; and you never knew when the next was due!

The V-2 was not as cost-effective as a bomber. Its accuracy gave it about a 50 per cent chance of hitting an eleven-mile circle at its maximum range. Some 1,358 V-2s were launched against England from The Hague, and over 400 hit London.

The V-2 and its motor had the following specifications:

V-2 specifications

V-2		Rocket	
Length	46 feet	Rocket fuel	Alcohol/oxygen
Width	12 feet (fins), 6 feet (body)	Length	7.9 feet
Height	56 miles (ceiling)	Maximum diameter	4.8 feet
Range	200 miles	Weight	28,000lb
Speed	3,600mph	Thrust	56,000lb
Control	Gyro and computer/radio		

Three strikes showed the V-2's capacity for destruction. On 25 November 1944 New Cross High Street was busy with shoppers in both Woolworths and the Co-op next door. Many queued outside Woolworths for saucepans that were on sale. At 12.26 p.m. there was an enormous explosion as a V-2 rocket hit the Woolworths store. The V-2 was seen in its last second of flight like a line across the grey sky.

This rocket caused the most awful tragedy in the V weapon campaign, and one of the worst civilian disasters of the Second World War. The store bulged outwards and then imploded. In the carnage 168 people died and 121 were seriously injured. The store erupted with a blinding flash of light and an enormous roar, followed by a dense cloud of smoke and dust. People several hundred yards away felt the warm blast on their faces, and some were physically pushed backward by its force. More people inside the Co-op were killed when that collapsed. The dead bodies of passers-by were also thrown great distances. An army lorry was overturned and destroyed, killing its soldiers, and a double-decker bus spun round causing even more deaths and injuries; its occupants were left still sitting in their seats covered in dust.

There were piles of masonry and pieces of bodies round the enormous gap where Woolworths had been. The devastation extended from the town hall to New Cross Gate station, and it took three days to clear this and retrieve the bodies from the debris. You will find undamaged pre-1944 buildings adjacent to those put up post-war in

1947. If you walk round the area you can see the V-2 strike boundary by the extent of the damage and its replacement. Lewisham council has since erected a blue plaque on the building to remember this tragedy.

Hughes Mansions were built in the 1920s in Vallance Road in Stepney. In 1945 many areas of East London still had many Jewish families and Hughes Mansions were no exception. At 07.20 hours on 25 March 1945, the day before Passover, a V-2 rocket struck the buildings. The names of the Jewish families killed in the flats are listed in the Jewish genealogical society website. Whole families were wiped out in the devastation when 134 people died. This was the second worst V weapon tragedy with a fatality rate only exceeded at New Cross. This is particularly poignant because it was the last day of the V-2 attacks, although it was not the last missile. That fell in Orpington killing one person.

Hughes Mansions were never rebuilt and the site is now a children's playground.

Ilford was hardest hit by the V-2. When a V-2 took off on 8 February 1945, Elsie Knight was ironing in her home at 1 Thorold Road, Ilford. At twenty-six, she and her two young sons were at home. The table at which she ironed stood under the back window. The V-2 reached the top of its parabolic flight in four minutes and then fell until it was doing its usual speed of 3,600mph when it hit Wright's Garage in Ley Street, about 200 yards from Elsie's home. The blast brought down ceilings, and blew out all the windows; the landing window being hurled, box frame and all, across the landing. No one in '1, Thorold' was injured, even the children's aunt, Vi, downstairs with her family. The families were evacuated to Sale in Cheshire and stayed with the Jarvises and the Waltons. If it had been a V-1 with its 1800lb warhead, against the V-2's 2,200lb, they would have all been killed, as V-1s flattened buildings over a wider area with their much lower impact speed. The high speed of the V-2 made it go deep before its blast was absorbed by the soil.

The V-2 not only destroyed Wright's Garage, but also the Super Cinema between Balfour Road and Ley Street, almost opposite Ilford Station. Fourteen people were killed. These were two cinema usherettes, seven working at the clothing factory opposite the cinema, one NFS fireman, and four local residents.

It could have been far worse for Britain if Hitler had successfully combined the V-2 with his attempts at making an atom bomb. Events like the allies' Telemark raids had greater consequences than appeared then. Even the prototype of a submarine-towed launching platform was made so that the United States mainland could have been devastated. Churchill's Hinge of Fate had swung against Hitler in the nick of time.

The V-3

The V-3 was basically a super gun. There would have been twenty-five of them and they would together have been able to fire ten rocket-assisted shells a minute at London. If this weapon had been used then London would have been completely evacuated.

Fortunately the V-3 was never fired. 617 Squadron, the Dam Busters, used Tallboy bombs to destroy the concrete dome covering the V-3 tunnels at Mimoyeques in Northern France, before the weapon could be used against London.

The Tallboy bomb is mentioned in W.J. Lawrence's book *No. 5 Bomber Group*, where he tells us that Barnes Wallis developed the Tallboy, the earthquake bomb of 1944, weighing 12,000lb and dropped from at least 20,000ft. It was extraordinary, an apparent contradiction in terms, since it had both the explosive force of a massive blast bomb and the penetrating power of an armour-piercing bomb. In ground tests it displaced a million cubic feet of earth and made a crater that it would have taken 5,000 tons of earth to fill. Ballistically perfect, it arrived faster than sound. So, in effect, it mimicked the V-2 rocket, when the noise of its arrival would be heard after the explosion. A simple calculation by the reader can verify the supersonic speed.

Of all the V weapons the V-3 was the least documented, mainly due to the fact that it was never used. It also seems that there was an official reluctance to discuss it after the war, probably due to the fact that British Intelligence had known little of the V-3. It was taken rather by surprise at its existence, so it was reluctant to admit it had failed to find the weapon. At least the RAF reacted quickly! It is only since official documents have been released into the public domain that we have known the whole truth about the V-3.

The Horten Flying Wing

The Second World War ended for British civilians once our armies had over-run the V-1 and V-2 sites. If our armies had been slower for any reason or unexpectedly held up after D-Day, we would have had to contend with another Nazi weapon in British skies, the Horten Flying Wing. Powered by two Junkers Jumo 004 jet engines, it was made invisible to radar by using a special coating. The Germans called it the '1000' bomber because it was designed to fly 1,000 kilometres, at 1,000 kilometres/hour and deliver 1,000 kilograms of bombs. It had a low drag configuration, ensuring that it could carry its bomb load as far as Birmingham at a speed faster than most British fighters, except the Gloster Meteor, which was powered by two Rolls-Royce jet engines. Thankfully this concept was never given time to enter active service even with the enthusiastic backing of Hermann Goering.

Epilogue

The chapter on German terror weapons prepares the way for this epilogue. The work of our Four Great Geniuses made an essential and underlying contribution to that terrible *Götterdämmerung* – the necessary final defeat of the Germans who had been wrongly led by the Nazis.

Our four weapons forged by the our Four Geniuses, radar, the Merlin engine, and the superb Hurricane and Spitfire aircraft, more than countered all that the Nazis could throw at us. Now thanks to them at last we could claim Victory over that evil system!

Bibliography

Bastow, D. (1989), *Henry Royce – Mechanic*, Rolls-Royce Heritage Trust.*

Birch, D. (1997), *Rolls-Royce and the Mustang*, Rolls-Royce Heritage Trust.*

Fighting Aircraft of World War II, Jane's Publishing Company 1946/47.

Fozard, Dr J.W. (1991), *Sydney Camm and the Hurricane*, Airlife Publishing.

Gordon, B. (1978), *Charlie Rolls – Pioneer Aviator*, Rolls-Royce Heritage Trust.*

Harvey-Bailey, A. (1985), *Rolls-Royce – Hives the Quiet Tiger*, Rolls-Royce Heritage Trust.*

Harvey-Bailey, A. (1992), *Hives' Turbulent Barons*, Rolls-Royce Heritage Trust.*

Harvey-Bailey, A. (1995) *The Merlin in Perspective – The Combat Years*, Rolls-Royce Heritage Trust.*

Jones, R.V. (1978), *Most Secret War: British Scientific Intelligence 1939–1945*, Hamish Hamilton.

Latham, B. and Stobbs, C. (1999), *Pioneers of Radar*, Sutton Publishing.

Mitchell, G. (2006), *R.J. Mitchell – Schooldays to Spitfire*, Tempus Publishing Ltd.

Price, A. and Blackah, P. (2007), *Supermarine Spitfire Owner's Manual*, Haynes Publishing.

Price, A. (2010), *The Spitfire Story*, Jane's Publishing Ltd.

Watson-Watt, R. (1957), *Three Steps to Victory*, Odhams Press.

Swords, S.S. (1986), *Technical History of the Beginnings of Radar*, IEE.

Museums and societies
RAF Museum, Hendon
Sir Robert Watson-Watt Society of Brechin

Websites
Wikipedia

*These books are from the Rolls-Royce Heritage Trust Historical Series. These books may be ordered from: The Rolls-Royce Heritage Trust, PO Box 31, Derby DE24 8BJ. Telephone: 01332 240 340.

Index

159

Bruneval 37–9
Brunsbuttel 23
Brush Electrical Engineering
	Company 52
Buckingham Palace 24
BUMF 87
Buzzard 62–3, 66, 124

C
Canadian aircraft 109
Canadian and Australian
	Navies 74
Canadian Hurricane 109
Canadian Hurricane Mk XIIAs
	106
Canewdon 8
Captain Biard 115, 118
Captain George Eyston 65
Castle Bromwich 135
'Cat' station 44
Cathedral of St Michael 34
cavity magnetron 45
CH (Chain Home) 8, 11–12, 17,
	22
CH calculations 10
Charles Stewart Rolls 51, 54–5,
	57–9
Charles Sykes 59
Charles Wright 71
CHEL (Chain Home Extra
	Low) 16
Cherbourg 31
CHL (Chain Home Low) 12,
	16, 23
Christian Hulsmeyer 6
Christopher Wren churches 27

Chromic acid bath 87
Churchill 19, 24, 35, 40, 146, 152
Clarendon Laboratory 26
Clark YH aerofoil 91–2
Claude Johnson 60–1
Cleves 31–2
Close-cowled BMW 139 89
Closed canopies 88
Clydebank 36
Co-op 150
Coastal Command 17, 43
'Cobber' Kain 100
Cody 113
Cologne 36, 41–3, 45, 79
Colonel Barrington 71
Colonel L.F.R. Fell 62
Colostomy 128
Commander Cook 38–9
Concorde 86
Condor 66, 89, 124
Confirmation 116
Constance Babington-Smith
	145
Controllability 82
Cook Street in Manchester 52
Cotton 138
Coventrate 35
Coventry 25, 32–6, 41, 44
Coventry Blitz 32
crane construction 53
Cranfield 149
Crewe 69–70
Cross-Channel flight 77–8
Crossed dipoles 9
CRT (cathode ray tube) 2, 7,
	9–12, 16, 42, 45